INSIGHT COMPACT GUIDES

BOSTON

GUIDES

Compact Guide: Boston is the perfect on-the-spot guide to the city that Oliver Wendell Holmes once called 'the thinking center of the continent, and therefore of the planet.' It tells you all you need to know about the attractions of Boston and Cambridge, from Beacon Hill to Back Bay, from Quincy Market to Harvard Square.

This is one of more than 70 titles in *Apa Publications'* new series of pocket-sized, easy-to-use guidebooks intended for the independent-minded traveler. *Compact Guides* pride themselves on being up-to-date and authoritative. They are in essence travel encyclopedias in miniature, designed to be comprehensive yet portable, as well as readable and reliable.

Star Attractions

An instant reference to some of Boston's most popular tourist attractions to help you on your way.

New State House p18

Quincy Market p21

Paul Revere House p24

USS Constitution p26

Public Garden p34

Harvard University p39

John Hancock Tower, Trinity Church p37

Boston Public Library p37

Lexington and Concord p44

Salem Witch Museum p49

Gloucester p51

Boston

Introduction

Places

Culture

Leisure

Practical Information

Boston – America's European City

Inevitably, visitors to Boston will hear the city and its environs called many things: 'the Athens of America,' 'the Hub of Universe' and the 'home of the bean and the cod.' These well-worn sobriquets still have a ring of truth, though most are based on legend. Few Bostonians even would argue that theirs is the nation's cultural or intellectual center as it was a century ago. New York City has seized the title and will not relinquish it. As for the bean and the cod, they may still be found, if only on souvenirs.

Old State House

Contemporary Boston is America's European City. It is so because of many things: its compact size and pedestrian-friendly streets; an architectural heritage spanning three centuries; for sidewalk cafés and cultural institutions. Moreover, Boston is an American city where tradition matters – a rarity in a nation that worships the new.

Education

In the first decade of English settlement, the Puritans laid the foundation of Boston's preeminence as a center of learning. Boston Latin School, the nation's first public school, was established in 1635. A year later, on the same day it passed legislation forbidding the sale of lace for garments, the Massachusetts General Court 'agreed to give £400 toward a schoale or colledge,' which was later named for John Harvard, a young minister who died in 1638 and bequeathed the new school in Cambridge half his estate as well as his library. In 1861, the Massachusetts Institute of Technology was granted its charter.

5

Today, dozens of schools and universities, public and private, dot the city. Boston University, where Martin Luther King studied philosophy and developed the nonviolent principles of the civil rights movements, is acclaimed as one of the nation's best city schools; Northeastern University is America's largest private school; and Boston College, under the administration of the Jesuit order, is one of the nation's finest Catholic institutions of higher learning. The strong student presence lends a youthful vigor to one of America's oldest metropolitan areas.

Puritan values aren't always shared by today's students

Medicine and Science

Boston's stature as a center of medical and scientific research also has roots in the Puritan era. Surprisingly, one of the men who encouraged the admittance of 'spectral evidence' in the Salem Witch Trials was also responsible for a significant medical breakthrough. In 1721, when a devastating smallpox epidemic struck Boston, the Rev. Cotton Mather, author of *The Wonders of the In-*

Dr John Collins Warren at work

visible World, a catalog of witchcraft and demonry, urged Boston's physicians to attempt the new and still heretical procedure of inoculation, which he had read about in English scientific journals. Only one, Dr Zabdiel Boylston, had the necessary courage, and despite threats from his colleagues, he successfully inoculated 250 people, including his six-year-old son.

In 1810, a committee led by Dr John Collins Warren raised funds from fellow Bostonians for construction of a public hospital. Thus, Massachusetts General was already a well-established institution in 1846 when Dr Warren performed the first operation under general anesthesia. More recently, Boston hospitals have performed a series of 'firsts' including the first kidney transplant at Brigham Hospital (1953); the first open heart surgery at Children's Hospital (1967); and development of artificial skin for burn victims (1981).

In other areas of science, too, Bostonians have made lasting contributions. Alexander Graham Bell and his assistant Thomas Watson developed the telephone in a Boston garret in 1876. In 1944, a team of scientists from Harvard, MIT and the US Navy developed the 'Mark I,' a digitally-programmed calculating machine more than 50 feet long, and ushered in the computer age. In Cambridge, Edwin Land built a tiny lens manufacturing company into a billion-dollar corporation and introduced the first Polaroid instant 'Land' camera there in 1947.

Literature

The first American printer in the English language was Stephen Day (or Daye) who published *The Bay Psalm Book*, a literal translation of Biblical psalms from the Hebrew, in Boston in 1640. In 1663, John Eliot, the 'Apostle to the Indians,' published a complete edition of the Old and New Testaments translated into the Algonquin tongue spoken by Massachusetts natives; it was the first Bible published in North America.

Ralph Waldo Emerson

Early Puritan laws requiring the elementary education of all children were intended so that a congregation might read scriptures. Reading and writing, however, quickly became a means to self-expression and, by the 1830s, Boston was hailed as the 'Athens of America.' Led by Ralph Waldo Emerson of Concord, local intellectuals nurtured the development of Transcendentalism, which indelibly shaped an emerging American social philosophy. One of the nation's first feminists, Margaret Fuller, was editor of *The Dial*, an influential literary journal that published work by Emerson, Henry David Thoreau and others. In Salem, Nathaniel Hawthorne completed *The House of Seven Gables* in 1851. *Walden*, Thoreau's musings on the simple life he led in a cabin at Walden Pond, Concord, appeared in 1854; it took the author five years to sell the 2,000 copies printed. Louisa May Alcott, another Concord resident who was raised with Emerson, Thoreau and Fuller as regular family guests, published Part I of *Little Women* in 1868.

Paradoxically for such a literary hotbed, Boston in the late 19th and early 20th centuries became best known for the censors of the New England Watch and Ward Society. Works by Ernest Hemingway, Sherwood Anderson and John Dos Passos, among others, were banned.

Architecture

Contributing to Boston's atmosphere as a 'European city' is its well-preserved collection of architectural styles dating to the late 17th century. On the Freedom Trail, the Paul Revere House, built of wood in 1680 in a simple style, is the city's oldest structure; the equestrian/patriot lived there from 1770 until 1800.

Paul Revere House

America's first trained architect, Charles Bulfinch, toured Europe from 1785 to 1787 at the suggestion of Thomas Jefferson, and was especially impressed by Georgian London. On his return to Boston, Bulfinch, barely 24, boldly submitted a plan for a new Massachusetts State House. His likely inspiration was London's Somerset House. Over the next several decades, Bulfinch designed important residences for many wealthy Boston families and completed drawings for the new Massachusetts General Hospital in 1816 before leaving for Washington, DC, and an assignment as architect of the US Capitol.

7

When Boston began filling in the Back Bay in 1857, the work sparked one of the city's most prolonged periods of real estate development. Today, the vast area between Boylston Street and Beacon Street from the Public Garden to Massachusetts Avenue is virtually an open-air museum of 19th-century residential architecture, predominantly brownstone townhouses. Boston's greatest architect of the period, Henry Hobson Richardson, was a Louisiana native who came to Harvard in 1855 as a student and remained in the area until 1876. Richardson's masterpiece is the Romanesque styled Trinity Church at Copley Square with stained-glass windows by Louis Tiffany and frescoes by John LaFarge.

Chestnut Street, Beacon Hill

Boston's built environment is superbly complemented by the Emerald Necklace. Designed by Frederick Law Olmsted, who also created the plans for New York City's Central Park, the Emerald Necklace was begun in 1881. The chain of thickets and open glades, brackish marshlands and freshwater ponds, wild forests and manicured flower beds stretches 5 miles from the urban confines of Boston Common to the open country of Franklin Park.

Boston's green lungs

In the first half of the 20th century, Boston's economic

John Hancock Tower behind
Boston Public Library

ills meant that much was preserved that might otherwise have been destroyed. Efforts in the late 1950s at so-called 'urban renewal' obliterated the West End and Scollay Square, replacing narrow streets and quaint structures with I.M. Pei's vast plaza of Government Center. A new City Hall (1968) in the stark brutalist style of Kallman, McKinnell & Knowles is admired by critics but disdained by citizens. The skyline was further shaped by I.M. Pei with the John Hancock Tower (1976), New England's tallest building. The International Style's other great practitioner, Philip Johnson, has contributed several buildings, most notably his addition to the Boston Public Library (1972).

Politics

America's great political dynasties – with the exception perhaps of New York's Roosevelts – are Masssachusetts families first. Vastly different in many ways, the Adams and Kennedy clans share at least a remarkable gift for passing through the generations a commitment to public service. Among his many titles, John Adams served his country as its first ambassador to Great Britain, as its first vice president and as the second president. Abigail Adams is remembered today not only as the wife and mother of a president (a unique distinction), but as the mother of American feminism; in 1776, she urged her husband to 'Remember the Ladies' at the fateful Continental Congress where independence was declared.

John and Abigail's son, John Quincy Adams, was not yet 27 years old when President Washington appointed him ambassador to the Netherlands; as Secretary of State under President James Monroe, Adams *fils* penned the Monroe Doctrine and succeeded Monroe to the White House. As President Lincoln's ambassador to Great Britain (the third generation of Adams men to serve at the Court

The State House circa 1801

of St James), Charles Francis Adams won the struggle to maintain that country's neutrality in the Civil War.

The Kennedys' line of public service comes through the Fitzgerald family. John 'Honey Fitz' Fitzgerald, father of Rose, was Boston's first Irish Catholic mayor. John Fitzgerald Kennedy, eldest son of Rose and Joseph Patrick Kennedy, an immensely successful businessman, entered politics at 29 when elected to the US Congress from a district taking in Cambridge and Charlestown. In 1960, 'JFK' became America's first Catholic president and, at 43, the youngest ever elected. His brother, Edward Moore 'Ted' Kennedy, went to the Senate in 1962 and has been re-elected ever since. When Joseph P. Kennedy III, son of Robert Kennedy, won his uncle's former congressional seat in 1986, the stage was set for yet another generation of Kennedys to be major actors in Boston politics.

The people's hero

Even Bostonians who never could have or would have voted for him remember 'His Honor' James Michael Curley as the city's quintessential politician. Born of poor Irish immigrants and orphaned at an early age, Curley epitomized the cultural clash of upstart Irish against entrenched Brahmins. He was elected Mayor of Boston four times, including a landslide victory in 1945 while under federal indictment for mail fraud. Later convicted, the 'Mayor of the Poor' insisted he had 'done it for a friend.'

9

Sports

As serious as Boston's reputation may seem, the city has all the same provided its share of athletic diversion to American culture. In 1863, the Oneida Football Club was formed by area students as the first such club in the United States and was never defeated in three years of play on the Boston Common. Over time, 'Boston rules' for football – liberally adapted from rugby and soccer – were adopted by American colleges.

In 1903, the Boston Pilgrims (later, the Boston Red Sox) of baseball's fledgling American League defeated the Pittsburgh Pirates in the first modern World Series. Boston's ace pitcher, Cy Young, was a 28-game winner in the regular season that year. Fenway Park opened in 1912 with a Red Sox victory against the New York Yankees, commencing a rivalry that continues unabated. Hometown hero George Herman 'Babe' Ruth combined remarkable pitching and hitting abilities and sparked the Red Sox's dominance of the majors between 1914 and 1918.

Red Auerbach, legendary coach of the Celtics basketball team
Backing the Bruins

Basketball was invented in Massachusetts at Springfield, and the Boston Celtics have until recently dominated play in the National Basketball Association. In 1995, the Celtics and the Boston Bruins of the National Hockey League moved from the legendary, if aging, Boston Garden to the sleek new FleetCenter.

Historical Highlights

1625 William Blackstone, a 29-year-old Anglican clergyman and Boston's first European settler, builds a log cabin on what is now Boston Common.

1630 John Winthrop, recently elected governor of the Massachusetts Bay Company, leads the *Arbella* and 10 other Puritan ships into Boston Harbor after a three-month trip from England.

1631 Boston court officials create America's first police force by putting watchmen on duty from sunset to sunrise.

1635 Boston Latin School, the nation's first public school, is founded.

1636 The Puritans show their commitment to education by founding a college at Newetowne, later Cambridge. It was subsequently to be named after its benefactor, John Harvard.

1640 Stephen Day, a locksmith and ironworker turns printer, publishes the first book produced in the colonies, *Bay Psalm Book*.

1660 A Quaker, Mary Dyer, is hanged on the Boston Common. The Quakers were denounced by Puritans as a 'cursed sect.'

1684 Massachusetts Bay Colony charter is revoked, ending Puritan independence from royal control.

1690 The first American newspaper, *Publick Occurrences: Both Foreign and Domestic*, is published in Boston.

1692 Salem Witch Trials begin.

1717 Boston Light, the oldest lighthouse in the nation, is erected in the harbor.

1761 Boston lawyer James Otis declares: 'Taxation without representation is tyranny.'

1764 Sugar Act and Stamp Act arouse anti-royalist sentiments.

1770 Boston Massacre, in which British troops fire on a rock-throwing mob, killing five.

1773 Phillis Wheatley, a young slave living with a wealthy Boston family, becomes the first published African-American poet.
Boston Tea Party, in which a shipment of tea is thrown into the harbor in protest against a new three-pence tax on tea.

1775 Paul Revere's ride and Battles of Lexington and Concord spark American Revolution.
Battle of Bunker Hill.
George Washington takes command of Continental Army at Cambridge.

1776 British troops evacuate Boston.
Declaration of Independence read from State House balcony.

1780 John Adams drafts Massachusetts Constitution including a Bill of Rights; John Hancock is first governor of the Commonwealth of Massachusetts.

1795 On Beacon Hill, Paul Revere and Samuel Adams lay cornerstone for the new State House by Charles Bulfinch, America's first professional architect.

1812 War of 1812 against British paralyzes city's commerce.

1814 American Industrial Revolution begins at Robert Cabot Lowell's first mill on the Charles River in Waltham.

1815 Handel & Haydn Society, now the nations's oldest continuously performing arts organization, gives its first concert.

1822 Boston is incorporated as a city.

1831 William Lloyd Garrison begins publishing an abolitionist journal, *The Liberator*.

1831 Mount Auburn Cemetery, the nation's first garden cemetery, opens in Cambridge.

1845 Henry David Thoreau begins living at Walden Pond.

1846 First operation under general anesthesia performed at Massachusetts General Hospital.

1852 Boston Public Library, the first free city library supported by taxes, opens.

1857 Filling of Back Bay begins, cleaning up a foul-smelling 580-acre public dump.

1861 Massachusetts Institute of Technology is granted charter.

1863 54th Massachusetts Voluntary Infantry, the first African-American regiment, is formed. Oneida Club first plays American-style football on Boston Common.

1868 Louisa May Alcott of Concord publishes *Little Women*.

1872 Great Fire of Boston destroys downtown, killing 33 people and razing 776 buildings.

1876 First words are spoken over telephone by Alexander Graham Bell.

1877 Swan boats launched at Public Garden.

1879 Radcliffe College founded for women.

1881 Boston Symphony Orchestra founded. Frederick Law Olmsted, landscape architect, begins work on Emerald Necklace park system.

1886 Henry James publishes *The Bostonians*.

1892 First Church of Christ, Scientist, established in Boston by Mary Baker Eddy.

1897 First Boston Marathon. First subway in America opens at Park Street.

1903 Boston Pilgrims defeat Pittsburgh Pirates in first baseball World Series.

1909 Filene's Automatic Bargain Basement opens in Washington Street.

1919 Strike of 1,300 Boston police. Breaking it brings Massachusetts Governor Calvin Coolidge to national prominence.

1920 Red Sox sell Babe Ruth to New York Yankees for $125,000.

1927 Italian immigrants Nicola Sacco and Bartolomeo Vanzetti are executed in a Charlestown prison for alleged killings and holdups. The case became a model for social injustice in the 1920s.

1942 Fire in a South Boston nightclub kills 490.

1944 The computer age dawns in Cambridge laboratories as a 50-ft-long calculating machine gets its sums right.

1945 James Michael Curley, although under indictment for fraud, wins fourth term as mayor.

1946 John Fitzgerald Kennedy, 29, elected to US Congress from Charlestown and Cambridge.

1947 Polaroid founder Edwin Land demonstrates first instant camera in Cambridge.

1950 A Brink's armored car is robbed in North End. Thieves net $2.7 million.. Eight men are convicted six years later.

1953 The world's first kidney transplant is performed at Brigham Hospital. The recipient lives for seven years.

1955 Martin Luther King is awarded a PhD from Boston University.

1959 The Boston Redevelopment Authority begins razing the old West End, long a center for gambling dens, burlesque halls and brothels but home to 7,000 people, and starts building Government Center and luxury apartments.

1962 The 'Boston Strangler' begins a 21-month rape and murder spree, killing 13 women.

1972 After 75 years as a men-only race, the Marathon acknowledges first women's winner.

1973 Robert Parker publishes *The Godwulf Manuscript*, the first 'Spenser' detective novel.

1978 A blizzard dumps 27.1 inches of snow on Boston and 48 inches in some parts of the state. Drifts in the city were as high as 15 ft.

1990 In the largest art heist in history, thieves remove $200 million in paintings from Isabella Stewart Gardner Museum.

1993 The TV series *Cheers*, set in a fictional Boston café, ends after 275 episodes.

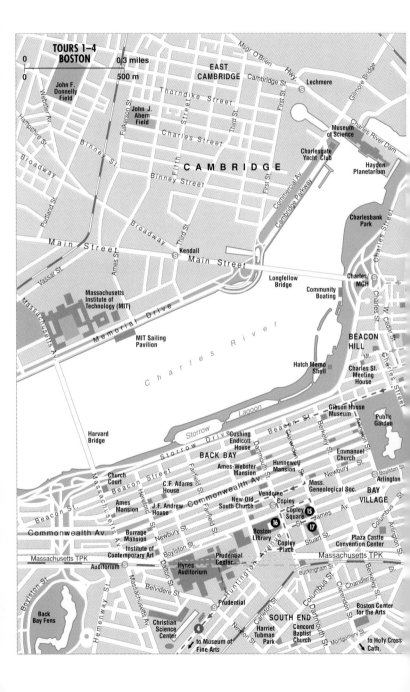

WHO DIED FOR THEIR COUNTRY
ON LAND AND SEA IN THE WAR
WHICH KEPT THE UNION WHOLE
DESTROYED SLAVERY
AND MAINTAINED THE CONSTITUTION
THE GRATEFUL CITY
HAS BUILT THIS MONUMENT
THAT THEIR EXAMPLE MAY SPEAK
TO COMING GENERATIONS

MARTIN MILMORE
SCULPTOR

Boston Common memorial

Tour 1

The Freedom Trail (Boston portion)
See map, pages 14–15

Crest on the Old State House
Freedom on the Common

The city's trademark attraction, the **Freedom Trail** is a 3-mile journey through the heart of Boston marked by a red line (sometimes painted, sometimes made of brick) that takes in 16 historic sites from **Boston Common** to the **Bunker Hill Monument** in Charlestown.

The official starting point is a **Visitor Information Center** on the Tremont Street side of Boston Common, about 150 yards from the Park Street MBTA subway station. It has free maps and tour information. Located directly opposite the **Old State House**, the **US National Park Service Visitor Center**, 15 State Street (tel: 242-5642) also has free maps and information as well as public restrooms. Free guided walking tours by Park Service Rangers are offered in spring, summer and fall. Eight of the Freedom Trail sites – Bunker Hill Monument, Charlestown Navy Yard, Faneuil Hall, Paul Revere House, Old North Church, Old State House, and Old South Meeting House – lie within the Boston National Historical Park.

In 1951, Boston newspaper reporter William Greenough Schofield conceived the idea of a 'Freedom Trail' in order to rescue tourists who otherwise became lost in the city's notoriously disorderly colonial-era streetscape. Contrary to legend, those meandering thoroughfares were not originally cow paths – though, at one time, Boston Common was the city's common pasture. The original nexus of Boston in the 17th century was an open-air market at what is now the Old State House, then a short walk from the town dock (various landfill projects have progressively extended the distance to the waterfront). As the

Puritan settlement grew, cobblestone paths radiated haphazardly from Great Street (now State Street). Modern urban planning was then unknown, of course; instead, this 'city in a wilderness' grew organically, like a tree pushing out new branches. If the early Bostonians gave any serious thought at all to how their new home should appear, they modeled it on the medieval English towns they had left behind.

A complete tour of the Freedom Trail may run anywhere from a one-hour express walk to a lingering one-day promenade, depending on one's energy and interests. By no means, however, does the Freedom Trail include every site worth visiting in the Cradle of Liberty. In fact, because it focuses almost exclusively on the Colonial and Revolutionary War periods, the Freedom Trail sometimes passes without a glance points of interest from relatively more recent times.

Soldiers and Sailors Monument, dedicated to the Union dead

17

In this book, two walking routes cover those sites as well as the stops on the Freedom Trail. The first route is confined to the central area of downtown Boston; the second takes in the North End and Charlestown.

★ ★ ★ **Boston Common**, where the Freedom Trail originates, is America's oldest public park of some 48 acres bounded by Park, Tremont, Boylston and Beacon streets. In 1630, the Common was created as a militia training grounds and 'for the feeding of Cattel' when the Puritans moved to Shawmut Peninsula from their original settlement at Charlestown. Troubled by a brackish water supply, they accepted the generous invitation of William Blackstone, then Shawmut's solitary settler, to share his 'excellent spring.' Blackstone lived here in a log cabin where he read his books and tended a vegetable garden and apple orchard. But, just as he had grown weary of 'the Lord Bishops' in England, so Blackstone soon grew tired of 'the Lord Brethren' in Boston. Preferring his own company, he left in 1624 and made a new settlement. He would likely have been appalled to learn that the Puritans later installed on his former homestead their gallows, stocks and pillory where criminals, Quakers and witches were punished and executed.

At the corner of Park and Tremont streets, the MBTA's **Park Street subway station** was opened in 1897. Boston's underground trolleys were the first in the US and were intended to clear a constant logjam of pedestrians and streetcars along Tremont Street. Originally, the subway ran just one stop to **Boylston Station**, also on the Common at the corner of Tremont and Boylston streets. **Central Burying Ground** ❶, at the Boylston Street edge of the Common, is the final resting place, in unmarked graves, of portrait painter Gilbert Stuart as well as British soldiers killed in Concord and at Bunker Hill.

Saying goodbye on Park Street

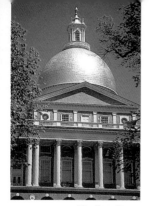

The State House

Immortalized in stone: General Joseph Hooker and JFK

Of the Common's several monuments, the most attractive – and arguably the most significant – commemorates the bravery of the African-American soldiers of the 54th Massachusetts Regiment. Called the ★ ★ ★ **Robert Gould Shaw Memorial** (corner of Park and Beacon Streets) after the white Bostonian of abolitionist parents who led the regiment and died with his men in an 1863 attack on Fort Wagner, South Carolina, it depicts Shaw on horseback surrounded by his troops. The relief sculpture by Augustus Saint-Gaudens powerfully evokes the Regiment's commitment to the cause of freedom.

On July 4, 1795, Massachusetts Governor Samuel Adams and fellow patriot Paul Revere laid the cornerstone for the 'new' ★ ★ ★ **State House** (tel: 727-3676 for information about free guided tours given daily). The site, on Beacon Street overlooking the Boston Common, was purchased from John Hancock whose mansion, since destroyed, stood nearby. The State House's principal entrance lies at the top of a flight of stairs, but there is also a public entrance at the Park Street side near the **statue of General Joseph Hooker**, a Civil War commander whose name will forever be linked – albeit erroneously – to the slang term for prostitutes. Beside him is the **statue of Mary Dyer**, who was hanged on the Boston Common in 1660 for her Quaker beliefs. On the opposite lawn, the **statue of John Fitzgerald Kennedy** calls up the gallant side of America's youngest president.

America's first professional architect, Charles Bulfinch, designed the red-brick and gold-domed State House when he was only 24 years old. He likely had for his inspiration Somerset House in London. For the construction of the new seat of government, the state legislature appropriated £8,000, but the final bill came to more than four times the original estimate. In return for their money, Massachusetts' citizens received a magnificent work of architecture. A late 19th-century amendment of yellow-bricked wings to either side of the Bulfinch structure prompted one critic to liken the State House to a ham sandwich; but, despite this and other alterations to the original design, the State House remains one of the country's finest public buildings.

Doric Hall, the main room on the ground floor, includes a portrait by Copley of General Thomas Gage, commander of British forces during the siege of Boston. The nearby **Hall of Flags** displays the standards of state regiments from various wars. In the House of Representatives hangs the '**sacred Codfish**,' a reminder of the importance Cape Cod fishery played in the early history of Massachusetts.

Return to the Boston Common at Park Street Station and cross Tremont Street to **St Paul's Cathedral-Episcopal ❷**, 138 Tremont (tel: 482-5800). The Greek Revival structure, by Alexander Parris (who also designed Quincy Market), was built in 1819–20; funds ran out before work for an entablature on the pediment could begin. At the corner of Tremont and Park Street, the 1809 **Park Street Church**, One Park Street (tel: 523-3383), was the last major Georgian church built in Boston. Its prominent steeple rises 217 ft. *America*, a hymn to the nation's 'spacious skies and amber waves of grain,' was first sung here on July 4, 1831.

Beside Park Street Church is the ★ ★ ★ **Old Granary Burying Ground ❸**, which takes its name from a public granary that stood here. Revolutionary War heroes John Hancock, Samuel Adams, Paul Revere, Robert Treat Paine and James Otis lie buried here along with the parents of Benjamin Franklin (marked by an obelisk in the center of the graveyard) and the victims of the Boston Massacre.

Continue along Tremont away from the Boston Common. On the opposite side of the street across from the Parker House Hotel at the corner of School Street is ★ ★ **King's Chapel ❹**, 58 Tremont Street (tel: 523-1749). Built in 1754 of Quincy granite, King's Chapel holds Paul Revere's largest bell, which is still in use. The severe, block-like exterior conceals a superb Georgian style nave. Boston's oldest graveyard, **King's Chapel Burying Ground**, includes among its permanent residents John Winthrop, first governor of Massachusetts, as well as Rev. John Cotton, a prominent Puritan minister, and architect Charles Bulfinch. A modern plaque marks the grave of Elizabeth Pain, who was imprisoned for adultery and may have been Nathaniel Hawthorne's inspiration for Hester Prynne in *The Scarlet Letter*.

School Street is so named because it was the site of the original Boston Latin School, the nation's oldest public school (the current school building is in the Fenway near Children's Hospital). A sidewalk plaque commemorating Latin's founding in 1635 is located directly in front of **Old City Hall**, designed in the French Second Empire style and completed in 1862. When city government offices were transferred to a 'new' City Hall in 1969, the building was threatened with demolition but was eventually rescued and restored with offices and a restaurant. In front, a **statue of Benjamin Franklin** honors a Latin School graduate who left Boston for Philadelphia in 1723.

At the corner of School and Washington streets is the well-preserved ★ **Globe Corner Bookstore**, 3 School Street (tel. 523-6658), dating from 1712. As the Old Corner Bookstore, it once housed Ticknor and Fields, the publishers of Hawthorne, Thoreau, Longfellow and Stowe. Between 1845 and 1865, the building was a meeting ground of literary giants and was lionized as 'the hub of the Hub' (as well as local lights, foreign guests included

Memorial at Old Granary

19

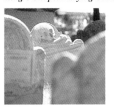

King's Chapel Burying Ground

Books ancient and modern

Old South Meeting House

The Old State House

The Boston Massacre

Dickens and Thackeray). After it had served as a pizza parlor in the 1960s, the building was restored by the Boston Globe company. Today, the Globe Corner Bookstore specializes in books on New England and travel.

Diagonally opposite the Globe Corner Bookstore is ★ ★ **Old South Meeting House ❺**, 310 Washington Street (tel: 482-6439). The Boston Tea Party began here on the night of December 16, 1773, when Sam Adams gave a signal during a meeting of the Sons of Liberty. The crowd began to whoop and make other warlike cries, then poured out into the streets and headed for the city's wharves. Old South, Boston's second oldest church, was built in 1729 by Congregationalists and during the siege of Boston was occupied by British troops, who converted it into a riding school by ripping out the pews and covering the floor with sand. The Great Fire of 1872, which devoured a 65-acre area from Washington Street to the waterfront, was stopped just outside its doors.

From the corner of Milk and Washington Streets, walk two blocks north to State Street and arrive at the back of the recently restored ★ ★ **Old State House ❻**, 206 Washington Street (tel: 720-3290) with permanent exhibits on the Revolutionary War period installed by the Bostonian Society, who lease the building from the city. Before entering, walk down State Street to the front end facing Congress Street in order to admire the figures of a lion and unicorn atop the gabled facade. These symbols of British royalty, which were removed in a peak of patriotic frenzy in 1776 and later replaced, recall the days when the royal governors of Massachusetts presided here, beginning in 1713. The building later served as the first State House and as Boston City Hall from 1831 to 1840.

Visitors should note that the **US National Park Service Visitor Center**, located directly opposite the Old State House at 15 State Street, has public restrooms, which are rare along the Freedom Trail.

On a traffic island in front of the Old State House is a **memorial to the Boston Massacre** at the site where an unruly mob confronted a band of trigger-happy redcoats on March 5, 1770 and five Bostonians fell dead. As they prepared to leave Boston for battle in the Civil War, the all-black 54th Regiment paused here to pay their respects to Crispus Attucks, an African-American who was among those killed in the massacre.

Follow Congress Street north one block. At the left-hand side is the back of the 'new' ★ **City Hall**, which was opened in 1969 following nearly a decade of controversial urban renewal that leveled Scollay Square, a famed vaudeville district, to make way for a **Government Center**, a complex of city, state and federal office buildings. Architects are nearly alone in their praise for City

Hall, a brick and concrete pile in the Brutalist style by Kallman, McKinnel & Knowles that Bostonians love to hate for its outlandish appearance (by local standards) and for its incomprehensible floor plans. An obscure plaque on City Hall Plaza notes that Alexander Graham Bell and Thomas Watson perfected the telephone in a building long since razed.

Much more to everyone's liking is ★ ★ ★ **Faneuil Hall**, on Congress Street opposite. Behind **a statue of Samuel Adams** with arms folded in determined opposition to British tyranny stands the familiar brick building with white cupola and grasshopper weather vane. Faneuil Hall was first built as a central market in 1742 with money donated by merchant Peter Faneuil (the French name recalls his Huguenot origins and may be pronounced either as *Fan'l* or *Fan-u-el*). Following a fire in 1761, it was rebuilt in the same design, then altered and enlarged by Bulfinch in 1805. The years leading up to the Revolutionary War heard speeches given here by James Otis and Samuel Adams, among others, and in the years after independence, Faneuil Hall hosted gala balls honoring Washington and Lafayette. On the first floor are shops and a US post office. The **Assembly Room** is dominated by a painting, *Liberty and Union, Now and Forever*, that shows Daniel Webster forcefully declaiming in the US Senate; the hall is still used today for political debates and citizenship ceremonies for naturalized immigrants.

Samuel Adams looks on

21

By 1822, when Boston was incorporated as a city, Bostonians had outgrown the market facilities provided at Faneuil Hall. Mayor Josiah Quincy, known as 'the great Mayor,' sought and won approval for a new market; his fellow citizens eventually named the market after him. ★ ★ ★ **Quincy Market**, directly behind Faneuil Hall, consists of three long and slender buildings designed by

Shopping at Quincy Market

Faneuil Hall Marketplace

Street entertainer

Alexander Parris in 1824. The **Central Building**, made of granite with a central, copper-clad rotunda, is flanked by the brick warehouses of **North Market** and **South Market**. In the early 1970s, following a long period of decline, the trio of historic buildings were restored and revitalized as a so-called 'festival marketplace,' bustling with shops, restaurants, comedy clubs and bars. The great success of the project led to its imitation across the US and around the world. Today, Faneuil Hall Marketplace is rivaled as a tourist attraction only by Disneyland and is visited by an estimated 50,000 people daily.

Return to the aisle between Faneuil Hall and Quincy Market, a popular performance space for musicians, mimes and jugglers, and cross North Street to Union Street. On a long traffic island between Congress and Union streets are ★★ **two statues** dedicated to James Michael Curley, who served four terms as Mayor of Boston, the first in 1914 and the last in 1945 (a race he won in a landslide while under federal indictment) as well as stints as Massachusetts Governor and US Congressman. The statues – one seated, the other standing – depict 'His Honor' in his dual role as man of the people and great orator.

Further down the island are a line of slender glass and steel towers that constitute Boston's newest public monument, the moving ★★ **Holocaust Memorial**.

Cross Union Street to the Union Oyster House, Boston's oldest restaurant, and turn right down Salt Lane into the **Blackstone Block** ❼. A compact collection of brick buildings and narrow alleys, this is one of Boston's oldest and most atmospheric districts. Street names such as Creek Square and Marsh Lane remind one that what is now dry land once lay on the water's edge. The brick building at 10 Marshall Street was constructed in 1760 by Thomas Hancock, John's uncle, and was later owned by John's brother, Ebenezer.

On the opposite side, at the corner of Salt Lane, the ★ **Boston Stone** lies at street level in a building foundation. Used as a paint mill and grinder in the early 18th century, the stone was laid here in 1737 by a tavern owner and later used as the point from which all distances to Boston were measured on roadside mile markers.

On Fridays and Saturdays, the Blackstone Block buzzes with the activity of the **Haymarket** when fishmongers, butchers and produce peddlers sell their goods and produce a kind of on-going street theater.

At the intersection of Hanover and Blackstone Streets, bronze reliefs of newspapers, food and other market detritus are imbedded into the street pavement. Called ★ *Asaraton*, from the ancient Greek for unswept floors, the sculpture is surely the city's oddest and most easily overlooked work of public art.

Tour 2

Paul Revere House

Freedom Trail: North End and Charlestown portion
See map, pages 14–15

23

This tour begins in the North End and concludes in Charlestown. Five Freedom Trail sites are located here, as well as other important points of interest.

To reach the North End, cross under the elevated Fitzgerald Expressway (also known as the 'Central Artery') through a pedestrian tunnel from Blackstone Street in Haymarket (*see facing page*) to the intersection of Salem and Cross Streets. Visitors and Bostonians can look forward to the eventual removal of the unsightly Central Artery, which will be replaced by an underground highway as part of a multi-billion-dollar road works project unlikely to be completed before the end of the century. In the meantime, expect the usual construction inconveniences and distractions throughout this part of downtown.

Those who prefer may travel directly to the Charlestown Navy Yard, where the *USS Constitution* is berthed, via the Route 93 MBTA bus from Haymarket station (one block from Blackstone Street at New Sudbury Street). In addition, a water shuttle operated by Boston Harbor Cruises (tel: 227-4320; $1 each way) leaves Long Wharf (between the Marriott Long Wharf Hotel and the New England Aquarium) for the Navy Yard every 30 minutes (every 15 minutes at weekday morning and evening rush hours).

Charlestown Navy Yard

North End café

North End

Virtually equated today with Italian cafés and restaurants, the North End's unique character and geographic isolation makes the area seem like an urban island. The **Central Artery**, constructed in the 1950s, has much to do with this, of course. The elevated roadway presents pedestrians with

a wall of girders, concrete and pavement that can be crossed only with great difficulty. Nevertheless, the district's isolation is historic. In the 17th century, the North End was linked to Shawmut Peninsula by a narrow neck (the present Blackstone Street) and was even known as the 'island of North Boston.'

From the 1820s, the North End has been a beachhead

The Italian influence

for waves of immigrant populations. First the Irish, then Eastern European Jews, and now Italians have found the North End an ideal setting to establish a distinctive American community with strong ties to the old country.

Exit the pedestrian walkway from Haymarket (*see above*), turn right on Cross Street, left on Hanover Street, right on Prince Street to North Square; this short walk passes by numerous cafés, restaurants and Italian specialty food shops. A trip to the North End really isn't complete without stopping for a cup of espresso in a café; a slice of pizza at **Pizzeria Regina**, 11½ Thatcher Street (tel: 227-0765); or a meal at any one of nearly two dozen restaurants from **Dom's**, 10 Bartlett Place (tel: 367-8979), where owner Dominic Caposella will sit with you and help you choose from his menu, to **The Daily Catch**, 323 Hanover Street (tel: 523-8567), where fresh fish dishes are a specialty. On summer weekends, the North End's narrows streets are crowded for the sort of colorful festivals and religious processions usually seen only on Italian soil.

24

Patriotic property of Paul Revere

A sightseeing tour through the North End traditionally begins at the ★ ★ ★ **Paul Revere House** ❽, 19 North Square (tel: 523-1676), which the famous patriot owned from 1770 to 1800. Built in 1680, the clapboard house with diamond-shaped casement windows is the oldest in Boston and lies behind a high wooden fence. A half-ton **bronze bell** – one of 200 Paul Revere bells – stands in the front courtyard. In addition to his well-known equestrian duties on April 18, 1775, Revere was a master silversmith, metallurgist and engraver of Huguenot descent (his father, Apollos de Rivoire, fled to Boston from France in 1715 and anglicized his name to Paul Revere). Exhibits inside the Revere House, which became a museum in 1907, include the **saddle bags** Revere used on his midnight ride plus a variety of 17th- and 18th-century furnishings.

Beside the Paul Revere House on the same grounds is the **Pierce-Hichborn House**, built in 1711 by Moses Pierce and now the oldest brick building in Boston. In 1781, Nathaniel Hichborn, Paul Revere's cousin, bought the house and it remained in the family until 1864.

St Stephen's Church

Backtrack to Hanover Street and turn right. ★ ★ **St Stephen's Church** ❾, 24 Clark Street (tel: 523-1230) is at the corner of Hanover and Clark Streets. Now a Roman Catholic church, St Stephen's was designed by

Charles Bulfinch and built in 1804 of red brick with a prominent white tower. This is Bulfinch's only surviving church in Boston, and was by turns a Congregational meeting house and the Second Unitarian Church of Boston until the Catholic Diocese purchased it in 1862.

Directly opposite St Stephen's is the ★ ★ ★ **Paul Revere Mall** ❿, also known as the **Prado**. Beneath an **equestrian statue** of Paul Revere by Cyrus Dallin, local residents gather to relax and share gossip (in English and Italian). Continue to the far end of the mall and across Unity Street.

Old North Church ⓫ (officially, Christ Church), 193 Salem Street (tel: 523-6676) is the oldest (1723) and most famous of all Boston churches. The famous steeple is actually the most recent in a series of replacements – it has fallen variously to hurricanes and fires. On April 18, 1775, as British troops began crossing the Charles to Cambridge, church sexton Robert Newman followed Paul Revere's orders and climbed the tower to hang two lanterns that could be seen in Charlestown as an alarm signal.

Old North Church

The church bells were cast in Gloucester, England and hung in 1745; as a young boy, Paul Revere was a member of a guild that agreed to ring the bells whenever the church warden so ordered. Inside the church, where Revere's descendants still maintain a family pew, is a **bust of George Washington** at the rear of the apse. On a visit in 1824, French General Lafayette, who served as the Virginian's aide-de-camp, admired the bust as 'more like him than any other portrait.'

25

At the entrance of Old North, facing Hull Street, walk straight to **Copp's Hill Burying Ground** ⓬ (1659), Boston's second oldest cemetery and named for William Copp, who farmed on the hill in the 1640s. Look for the impressions of musket balls on many of the tombstones that were left when British troops practiced their marksmanship here in the Revolutionary War period.

Copp's Hill Burying Ground

Near the gate at the Charter Street edge of the cemetery is the **Mather tomb**, last resting place of Increase and Cotton Mather, father and son, as well as numerous others in the famous family of Puritan ministers. Cotton Mather is remembered for helping incite the Salem 'Witch Trials' in 1692 – he wrote *The Wonders of the Invisible World*, a catalog of witchcraft and demonry – but Mather also helped urge a great advance in science when he convinced Boston physician Zabdiel Boylston to use inoculation as a way to protect citizens during a 1721 smallpox epidemic (the minister had read about inoculation theory in English scientific journals). The corner of the graveyard at Snowhill Street was the **precinct for deceased blacks**, including Prince Hall, first grand master of the African Grand Lodge of Masons in Massachusetts.

Historic Charlestown

Charlestown

From Copp's Hill Burying Ground, follow Charter Street to Commercial Street and cross to the water's edge. Turn left and continue several blocks to Endicott Street and the Boston side of the Charlestown bridge. Turn right and cross the bridge, which lies over the terminus of a series of locks linking the Charles River with Boston Harbor. The red line of the Freedom Trail as well as a series of signs will direct you along Water Street to the *USS Constitution* and the Charlestown Navy Yard through an otherwise uninteresting (to a degree even unappealing) district of warehouses and highway exit ramps.

As previously mentioned, a water shuttle operated by Boston Harbor Cruises (tel: 227-4320; $1 each way) leaves Long Wharf (between the Marriott Long Wharf Hotel and the New England Aquarium) for the Navy Yard every 30 minutes (every 15 minutes at weekday morning and evening rush hours). The short harbor trip represents an attractive alternative to walking.

26

The ★ ★ ★ **Charlestown Navy Yard** (tel: 242-5601) was for over 160 years one of the country's most important naval centers, from its opening during the War of 1812 to its closing in 1974 as the Vietnam War drew to an end. Perhaps the most unusual structure on the 30-acre site is the quarter-mile **rope-walk**, where ships' cordage was produced; it was designed by Alexander Parris, architect of Quincy Market, and completed in 1837.

The Charlestown Navy Yard's prime attraction is the ★ ★ ★ **USS** *Constitution* (tel: 242-5670), the oldest commissioned ship in the US Navy (bicentennial anniversary: 1997). Navy seamen dressed in uniforms from the War of 1812 lead guided tours daily.

Built in Boston at the Hartt Brothers Shipyard in 1797, the *Constitution* was the largest American warship of its

On guard at Constitution Wharf

USS Constitution

time and typically carried more than 50 massive guns. At 204 ft long and with a displacement of 2,200 tons, the great frigate was longer and heavier than any other ship of its kind. Paul Revere cast the bolts fastening its timbers as well as the copper sheathing for the boat's bottom. In 40 battles, the *Constitution* always emerged victorious.

When Congress declared war against the Barbary States of North Africa in 1802, the *Constitution* played a leading role in the blockade and bombardment of Tripoli. When Congress again declared war in 1812, this time against the British, the ship gained immortal fame in a contest with the Royal Navy frigate *Guerrière*. During a duel that saw the two ships approach within pistol firing range, a British cannonball appeared to bounce off the *Constitution*. 'Good God,' an American sailor exclaimed, 'her sides are made of iron!' An hour later, the *Guerrière* surrendered and the *Constitution* became legendary as 'Old Ironsides.' When it faced scrapping in 1828, Oliver Wendell Holmes led a public drive to save the ship; his poem, *Old Ironsides*, moved Congress to restore and recommission the *Constitution* for diplomatic duty. The ship was rescued again in the late 1920s and has been permanently berthed at the Charlestown Navy Yard ever since. On July 4, the ship takes a majestic turn in Boston Harbor so that its hardy hull will weather evenly.

The Constitution in close-up

The floating companion of 'Old Ironsides' is the **USS Cassin Young**, a decommissioned World War II destroyer also open daily for tours. The ★★ **USS Constitution Museum** (tel: 426-1812) details the ship's history and the lives of its sailors. A variety of ship's models and paintings of clippers ships are displayed at the nearby **Boston Marine Society** (tel: 242-0522).

Pick up the red line of the Freedom Trail outside of the Navy Yard and follow it up Monument Avenue to the 221-ft-high ★★★ **Bunker Hill Monument** (tel: 242-5641), dedicated on July 17, 1843 by President John Tyler. Daniel Webster, Tyler's Secretary of State, delivered a thundering oration to a crowd of 100,000. Vigorous visitors can ascend the monument's 294 steps for a view of Charlestown and Boston harbor (there is no elevator). A museum at the base includes several dioramas depicting one of the first major battles in the Revolutionary War.

By now, almost everyone knows that the Battle of Bunker Hill, as well as the monument, are located on Breed's Hill. The fault, if that's the proper word, lies with Colonel William Prescott and his men who were ordered on June 16, 1775 by General Artemus Ward of the Continental Army to fortify Bunker Hill, but chose instead to dig in at Breed's. This was probably not accidental, for Breed's Hill was shorter and lay closer to Boston than

27

Bunker Hill Monument

Bunker Hill. What the Yankees sought was a commanding position overlooking Boston harbor; for their pains, they attracted punishing shelling by the British fleet on the morning of June 17. Later, a force of 1,500 redcoats landed at Charlestown and set fire to the nearly deserted district.

When the British began a charge up Breed's Hill that afternoon, the Yankees held their fire until the enemy came within 50 feet. The delaying tactic was prompted by a need to conserve ammunition, but it has given rise to the legend that Colonel Prescott ordered his men, 'Don't fire till you see the whites of their eyes!' In fact, the remark was already something of a military cliché, and was probably first made at least 30 years earlier by a Prussian prince.

The Battle of Bunker Hill

The Battle of Bunker Hill took a bloody toll on both sides. Among the 140 Americans who died was Dr Joseph Warren, recently commissioned a major-general; Major John Pitcairn fell along with 225 other redcoats. Wounded were 271 Americans and 828 British.

Designed by Simon Willard and built of Quincy Granite, the Bunker Hill Monument's cornerstone was laid on June 17, 1825 (the 50th anniversary of the battle) by General Lafayette. Funding and engineering problems caused interminable construction delays over the next 13 years. In fact, it even became necessary to construct a private railway for horse-drawn carts – America's first commercial railway – to haul from Quincy to Boston the extraordinarily heavy blocks called for in Willard's design (the pyramid-shaped cap alone weighs 5,000 pounds).

28

Serving across the centuries

Descend Monument Avenue to Warren Street, turn right and take the next left onto Pleasant Street. The three-story **Warren Tavern**, 2 Pleasant Street (tel: 241-8142) is the oldest tavern in Boston (built in 1780 after the Charlestown fire) and was named for the fallen hero of the Battle of Bunker Hill. Among the patriots who once stopped here were Paul Revere and General George Washington.

Where Warren Street meets Main Street at Thompson Square, continue to Phipps Street on the left and turn in to the ★ **Phipps Street Burying Ground**, which provides the best historical record of pre-revolutionary Charlestown thanks to its unique layout: families were buried in rectangular plots corresponding to the locations of their homes. Although John Harvard is not actually buried here, an obelisk commemorating the preacher was erected in 1828 by Harvard alumni. When he died in 1638, he left his books and half his estate to a new college established by the Puritans which was later named in his honor. Many of Boston's first generation of settlers are also buried in the cemetery; at least 100 graves date from before 1700.

You can now return to the center of Boston via the water shuttle from the Navy Yard.

Tour 3

Beacon Hill *See map, pages 14–15*

In 1630, the most prominent feature of Shawmut Peninsula was Trimountaine, so named for its three peaks: Pemberton, Beacon and Mount Vernon (looking from east to west). Today, only a truncated Beacon Hill survives, with the others leveled for various landfill projects that accommodated Boston's swelling population in the 18th and 19th centuries.

As early as 1634, an act of legislation designated Beacon Hill as a sentry spot, and a torch was left blazing there to guide ships safely into Boston Harbor. Beacon Hill began to acquire its current appearance in 1795, when Samuel Adams, then Massachusetts governor, and Paul Revere laid the cornerstone for a new State House designed by Charles Bulfinch. Shortly afterward, Harrison Gray Otis and other prominent local merchants formed the Mount Vernon Proprietors to buy and develop land in the surrounding area. They began with a vast parcel owned by artist John Singleton Copley, making for the largest land transaction in Boston up to that time, covering an area enclosed by Beacon Street, Walnut Street, Mount Vernon Street to Louisbourg Square, down Pinckney to what was then the Charles River and along its bank to Beacon Street. The Proprietors immediately began to lay out streets and construct a series of mansions and townhouses which form an architectural legacy equaled in Boston only by the later development of Back Bay.

Beacon Hill is noteworthy not only for its buildings, however, but also for its inhabitants. If Boston was indeed the Athens of America in the 19th century, then 'the hill' was its Mount Olympus, home to such towering figures as Henry Adams, Louisa May Alcott, William Dean How-

Dignified Beacon Hill

29

Homing in on the Hill

High-class homes on the Hill

Just resting on Joy Street

ells, and Francis Parkman. The American Unitarian Association was formed here in 1825, and Unitarians on Beacon Hill and elsewhere played a large role in shaping the moral character of Bostonians. The Brahmins, as they became known, were serious, prosperous, and thoroughly patrician, yet among them were abolitionists, philosophers, and numerous men and women of *belles lettres*.

From the State House, Beacon Street slopes to the west along the edge of the Boston Common. The **Unitarian Universalist Association**, a successor to the American Unitarian Association, has its offices at 25 Beacon Street (tel: 742-2100); its bookstore sells a full line of volumes from the UUA-owned Beacon Press. Joy Street, at the first crosswalk, dates from 1661 and is one of Boston's oldest streets. At 5 Joy Street are the headquarters of the **Appalachian Mountain Club** (tel: 523-0636), which maintains trails and shelters for hikers and mountaineers following the Appalachian Trail through the White Mountains of New Hampshire and elsewhere in New England.

Designed by Alexander Parris, architect of Quincy Market, the twin structures at 39 and 40 Beacon Street were built in 1819 for, respectively, merchant Nathan Appleton and Daniel Pinckney Parker, who owned stock in the Lowell mill concerns. Parris also designed the adjacent Sears Mansion, 42 Beacon Street, which is now the library and rooms of the exclusive **Somerset Club** (tel: 227-1731). Here and elsewhere, original window panes are tinted purple from impurities in the glass that were sensitive to sunlight.

In 1806, Harrison Gray Otis – whose long career of public service included terms as US Senator and Mayor of Boston – moved into ★ ★ **45 Beacon Street**, the third in a trio of homes by Charles Bulfinch he commissioned over nine years. The current occupants, the American Meteorological Society (tel: 227-2425), are required under the terms of their lease to show the mansion, where Otis entertained President James Monroe and many others, to anyone who so inquires.

Before turning up Spruce Street, take note of a plaque at 50 Beacon Street that recalls the memory of the 'Rev. William Blaxton,' who is credited as 'first settler of Shawmut 1625. Near here stood his dwelling… The Place of his Seclusion became a Great City.' Blackstone, as his name is usually written, was a graduate of Emanuel College and member of a failed colony near what is now Weymouth. In 1625, he agreed with the local inhabitants to take possession of the Shawmut peninsula, where he lived alone with his books and a vegetable garden until the arrival of the Puritans.

Turn right on Spruce Street, then left on Chestnut Street,

which along with Mt Vernon Street are the architectural crown jewels of Beacon Hill. During the Civil War Period, Dr Samuel Gridley Howe, founder of the Perkins Institute for the Blind, and his wife, author Julia Ward Howe, lived at ★ ★ **13 Chestnut Street**. In addition to their formidable professional careers, the couple were ardent abolitionists; Mrs Howe wrote the words to *The Battle Hymn of the Republic*, the rousing Union marching song. This house and numbers 15 and 17 were designed and built by Charles Bulfinch between 1816 and 1818. The brick facade, black shutters, and white columns at the entrances are quintessential Beacon Hill features.

Ubiquitous antiques

The oldest home (1799) on the south slope of Beacon Hill is ★ **29A Chestnut Street**, also by Bulfinch; the actor Edwin Booth, brother of Lincoln's assassin John Wilkes Booth, lived here in the 1880s. The historian Francis Parkman lived at **50 Chestnut Street** from 1865 until 1893.

At the bottom of Chestnut Street is Charles Street, the commercial center of Beacon Hill. The street is lined with fashionable restaurants and eclectic antique shops. At the corner of Charles and Mt Vernon Streets, the **Charles Street Meeting House** was built from a design by Asher Benjamin as the Third Baptist Church. In 1807, the Charles River came near the church doorstep and baptisms were performed in its waters. Today, the church building is used for stores and offices.

Beacon Hill's finest homes line ★ ★ **Mt Vernon Street**, which Henry James satirically tagged as 'the only respectable street in America.' For many visitors today, ★ ★ ★ **Louisburg Square** (pronounced *Lew-is-burg*) is the high point of a Beacon Hill tour. The square's centerpiece, a private park enclosed by a wrought-iron fence, is maintained by owners of the surrounding townhouses, who comprised the first home association in the United States. Statues of Columbus and Aristides the Just were donated in 1850 by Joseph Iasigi, a Greek merchant. Louisburg Square and its cobblestone streets have welcomed numerous famous residents in over a century and a half. The area was named for the Siege of Louisburg, a Nova Scotia fortress captured by Massachusetts militiamen in 1754. In another time, William Dean Howells, novelist and editor of the *Atlantic Monthly*, lived at No. 4; Louisa May Alcott moved her parents and sisters to No. 10 after her success with *Little Women*; in 1852, Jenny Lind, the 'Swedish Nightingale,' was married at No. 20 to her accompanist.

The ★ ★ **'Second Otis House'** at 85 Mt Vernon Street, a three-story mansion with cobblestone drive, was built by Bulfinch in 1800–02. His dream for a group of freestanding homes never materialized. Henry Adams, author

31

Louisburg Square

The 'Second Otis House'

Knocking on wood

62 Pinckney Street

and historian, grew up at **57 Mt Vernon Street**, another of Bulfinch's distinguished contributions to this district. At the top of the hill, the ★ **Nichols House Museum**, 55 Mt Vernon Street (tel: 227-6993), is the only private house museum to be found on Beacon Hill; Rose Nichols, the niece of Augustus Saint-Gaudens and a writer and landscape architect who died in 1960, was its last resident. The facade has not been altered since it was constructed by Bulfinch in 1804.

At the crest of Mt Vernon Street, turn left on Joy Street toward the '**North Slope**' of Beacon Hill, which was a predominantly African-American area in the 18th and 19th centuries. Many of the homes here are listed on Boston's **Black Heritage Trail**. On Pinckney Street, No. 62 was a stop on the '**Underground Railway**,' a chain of safe houses for slaves fleeing the South to freedom in Canada before the Civil War (even though Massachusetts and other Northern states had abolished slavery, the Fugitive Slave Act permitted the arrest and return of escaped blacks). In 1920, workers uncovered a secret attic chamber here, as well as a tin plate and two iron spoons.

The **John J. Smith House**, 86 Pinckney Street, is named for a free black from Virginia whose barbershop at the site was a popular meeting place for African-American abolitionists. In 1878, Smith became the first African-American appointed to the Boston Common Council.

Backtrack to Joy Street, but pause at 24 Pinckney Street to see why it is known as the '**House of Odd Windows**' (each one is different, from a roof-top 'eyelid' window to a small square window beside the front door). Turn left on Joy Street and descend to **Smith Court**. The **Abiel Smith School**, 46 Joy Street, was dedicated in 1834 for the education of African-Americans, but was closed 10 years later when Boston's public schools became racially

Pooches on Pinckney Street

integrated. Today, the school contains the offices of the
★ ★ ★ **Museum of Afro-American History**  (tel: 742-
1854), which maintains its exhibits at the neighboring
African Meeting House, 8 Smith Court (tel: 742-5415).
Dedicated in 1806, the African Meeting House is the oldest African-American church still standing. It was known
as the 'haven from the loft' because black worshippers
at Old North Church were confined to the loft. In 1832,
William Lloyd Garrison, publisher of *The Liberator*,
founded the New England Anti-Slavery Society here.

At the bottom of Joy Street, cross Cambridge Street and
turn right to the headquarters of the Society for the Preser-
vation of New England Antiquities (SPNEA), located in
the distinguished ★ ★ **First Harrison Gray Otis House**
, 141 Cambridge Street (tel: 227-3956). It is a sym-
metrical three-story block of red bricks, with each story
being defined by a brownstone string course. The first two
floors are a museum with all furnishings, including the
wallpaper, faithfully accurate to Federal Period detail. Re-
markably, the now elegant house was used as a ladies'
Turkish bath in the 1830s.

First Harrison Gray Otis House

Old West Church, 131 Cambridge Street (tel: 227-
5088) was designed by Asher Benjamin in 1806 and is a
Methodist church. A predecessor was destroyed in 1775
when the British thought the Americans were using its
steeple to signal to their compatriots in Cambridge. Formerly known as the West End, the area behind and beside the church and Otis House was razed in the late 1950s
for an urban renewal project that created the nearby Government Center and several high-rise apartment towers.

Old West Church

33

Backtrack along Cambridge Street toward the Charles
River. Turn right on Grove Street, then left on to Fruit
Street to the complex that constitutes Massachusetts General Hospital and the grey-bricked **George R. White
Memorial Building** with its landmark bay window tower.
In 1810, a committee led by Dr John Collins Warren raised
more than $100,000 for construction of a public hospi-
tal; today, 'MGH' is an internationally recognized medical institution.

Inside the hospital's main entrance, ask directions to the
★ **Bulfinch Pavilion and Ether Dome**, Bulfinch's last
Boston commission before he departed to become architect of the US Capitol. In the domed operating theater il-
luminated by a skylight, Dr Warren performed the first
surgery under general anaesthesia on October 16, 1846
with ether administered by William Thomas Green Mor-
ton. Following the procedure, the patient, who had been
suffering from a tumor on his jaw, asserted he had felt
no pain. In a typical proper Bostonian understatement,
Dr Warren declared to his colleagues: 'Gentlemen, this
is no humbug.'

Tour 4

Back Bay *See map, pages 14–15*

Back Bay blooms

The botanical bounty of the Public Garden, the elegant brownstones that line Marlborough Street, and the shops, galleries and cafés colorfully strung along Newbury Street lend this section of Boston a distinctly Parisian air. Baron Haussmann would certainly have recognized kindred spirits in the 19th-century planners who laid out the neat, tree-lined grid of Back Bay's streets and avenues. Unlike older areas of the city, where the Puritans' cows are blamed for the idiosyncratic streetscape, Back Bay is orderly and rectangular. Sharp-eyed visitors will even notice that the principal streets running north-south from the Public Garden were named alphabetically, so that Arlington precedes Berkeley, and so on, ending at Hereford.

Today's lovely area was an odorous eyesore a century and a half ago. Boston's original settlement clung to the Shawmut peninsula, a roughly circular clump of hills joined to the mainland by a narrow natural causeway. Tidal marshes of the surrounding Charles River estuary ran up to the back edge of the Boston Common, hence the name, 'Back Bay.' In 1813, the Mill Dam was constructed across the Back Bay's northern edge to supply power for mills in South Boston. As an consequence, Back Bay was drained every day, exposing the land to the sun and other elements. Bostonians were also unable to resist the human urge to dump garbage and other waste where they believed no one would notice. But people did take horrified notice; the smell, the putrefaction and the rats were appalling.

The first improvement began just beyond the Boston Common in 1839 with development of the ★ ★ ★ **Public Garden**. The oldest botanical garden in the United States, it is lovingly planted with all manner of flora from tulips in spring to a selection of tropical palms at the height of summer. In spring and summer, Boston youths pedal the legendary 'swan boats' around the Garden's small pond while resident ducks trail beside in the water seeking food. A picturesque suspension bridge, supposedly the world's shortest, crosses the pond at its center.

Just inside the park's entrance at the corner of Charles and Beacon streets are a set of bronze statues depicting the Mallard family of *Make Way For Ducklings*, Robert Mc-Closkey's classic children's book. Small children adore clambering over the eight ducklings or riding on Mrs Mallard's back. Elsewhere in the park, statues of interest include that of Edward Everett Hale, author of *The Man Without a Country* (at the Charles Street entrance opposite the Boston Common), and Charles Sumner, who led abolitionist forces in the US Senate before the Civil War

Swanning around

Mounted on Mrs Mallard

34

(on the Public Garden's Boylston Street perimeter). Near the park's Commonwealth Avenue entrance on the Arlington Street perimeter is the Ether Monument, commemorating the first use of general anesthesia at Massachusetts General Hospital in 1846.

Cheers – time for a drink

35

Facing the Public Garden is the ★ ★ **Bull and Finch Pub**, 84 Beacon Street (tel. 227-9605), the inspirational setting for *Cheers*, the long-running television sitcom. The interior doesn't resemble the studio set in any way, but that detail doesn't deter the numerous out-of-towners who still flock here several years after the show's 10-year run ended.

A heroic statue of General George Washington on horseback faces the 200-ft wide ★ ★ **Commonwealth Avenue Mall**, first link in the Emerald Necklace chain of green spaces. Imposing Victorian mansions and former hotels line either side of the mall. For a limited view of their grand interiors, step inside the headquarters of the Boston Center for Adult Education, 5 Commonwealth Avenue. The **Ritz-Carlton**, 15 Arlington Street (tel. 536-5700), opened in 1927 as the nation's first Ritz, has a fairly formal lounge with a splendid view of the Public Garden; ditto for the Bristol Lounge of the **Four Seasons Hotel**, 200 Boylston Street (tel. 338-4400).

Commonwealth Avenue Mall

Immediately following the Public Garden's construction, Boston officials focused attention on remaining land in Back Bay as a site for real estate speculation. In 1849, the area was conveniently declared a health hazard and a committee appointed to determine a solution. Fantasy-filled design proposals included an artificial lake, and circus grounds to be built on an artificial island in the Charles.

In 1857, commissioners approved a development plan that extended Boylston and Beacon streets to the west and created Commonwealth Avenue as well as Newbury and Marlborough Street. The state contracted for removal of land from Pemberton Hill (one of the hills in the original Trimountain, along with Beacon Hill and Mount Vernon) as well as for the hauling of gravel by railroad from Needham. Sale of developable lots would pay for the ambitious public works project.

The Victorian Society of America maintains the 1859 ★ **Gibson House Museum**, 137 Beacon Street (tel. 267-6338), one of the first Back Bay mansions built and the only one offering guided tours (weekends only). The sumptuously furnished dining room is set with a Rockingham service and English Regency chairs. Among the first of Boston's elite to move into Back Bay were John and Isabella ('Belle') Gardner, who were married in 1859. At **150 Beacon Street**, they built a mansion on a lot that was a wedding gift from Belle's father. In 1859, trains up to 35 cars long, each loaded with landfill material, arrived in Back Bay every 45 minutes, day and night. Construction work continued well into the 1880s. Perhaps the musicians playing in Mrs Gardner's Parisian-style drawing room helped to drown out the din.

Turn left on Clarendon Street and cross Marlborough Street, one of Back Bay's most attractive residential streets. At the corner of Commonwealth Avenue, the **First Baptist Church**, 110 Commonwealth Avenue (tel. 267-3148) was the first important commission of architect Henry Hobson Richardson. The church's prominent tower is surmounted by a bas relief of trumpeting angels, sculpted in Paris after Richardson's design by Frédéric-Auguste Bartholdi, better known for the Statue of Liberty.

First Baptist Church

Continue south on Clarendon to **Newbury Street**, crowded from Arlington Street to Massachusetts Avenue with art galleries, chic boutiques, restaurants and sidewalk cafés. On Sundays, an orchestra and chorus perform Bach cantatas at ★ **Emmanuel Church**, 15 Newbury Street (tel. 536-3355). A distinguished Boston clothier, **Louis Boston**, 234 Berkeley Street (corner of Newbury Street), displays its wares in the former home of the Museum of Natural History, built in 1864, and later succeeded by the Museum of Science. The original site of the Massachusetts Institute of Technology, founded in 1861, stood beside it; the current structure is headquarters of the New England Insurance Company with historical murals in its lobby.

Newbury Street mural

At the south end of Louis Boston is **Boylston Street**, one of the city's busiest thoroughfares of office towers and stores. A huge bronze bear announces the presence of **FAO Schwarz**, the famous toy store, at 440 Boylston Street.

Waterstone's Booksellers, 26 Exeter Street at the corner of Newbury Street (tel. 859-7300), was originally the 'Temple of Working Union of Progressive Spiritualists,' built in 1884, and converted to a theater in 1914.

Backtrack to Dartmouth Street and walk one block south to Boylston Street at Copley Square. At the corner

Bear necessities for kids

36

of Clarendon and Boylston streets, stands ★ ★ ★ **Trinity Church ⓯**, frequently nominated as one of the 10 finest buildings in the US. Designed by H. H. Richardson in 1872 and completed in 1877, Trinity's French Romanesque form recalls a sybaritic king seated on his throne. The great bulk of the church's granite foundation supports a broad, imposing tower with a simple crown. The building's heavy robes of stone – granite decorated with a ruddy freestone – are richly embroidered with statuary and flecked with the baubles of John LaFarge's stained-glass windows.

Trinity Church

Inside, Trinity is a feast of painting and decoration. La-Farge and assistants including Augustus Saint-Gaudens achieved the first large-scale frescoes ever attempted in the US. The panels depict a variety of Old and New Testament scenes. LaFarge also designed the majority of Trinity's dazzling stained-glass windows; 'Christ in the Act of Benediction,' a three-paneled window in the west wall of the nave, would be especially inspiring for any minister preaching from the white marble pulpit.

Lunching in the park

Setting off Trinity's intricate is the open space of **Copley Square Park**, named for artist John Singleton Copley (1738–1815), who enjoyed a reputation for the sharpest eye of any painter in the colonies and counted Samuel Adams and Paul Revere among his clients. Facing Trinity Church on the park's Dartmouth Street perimeter is the original ★ ★ ★ **Boston Public Library ⓰**, designed in the Renaissance Revival style by McKim, Mead and White and opened in 1895. Recent extensive renovations have reinvigorated the palatial interior, which includes murals on Judaism and Christianity by John Singer Sargent, among others. A courtyard with garden and chairs allows one to imagine having stepped from 20th-century Boston into 16th-century Italy. It's back to the austere modern world once again, inside the library's 1972 addition by Philip Johnson, whose main entrance at 500 Boylston Street is also the finish line of the Boston Marathon.

Boston Public Library

Completing the triumphal architectural triumvirate of Copley Square is ★ ★ **New Old South Church**, 645 Boylston Street (so named because the congregation, Boston's third oldest, moved in 1875 to Back Bay from its 1729 home at Old South Meeting House, 310 Washington Street). New Old South's Italian cookie wafer facade in Roxbury puddingstone makes for an exuberant display of the principles of Ruskinian Gothic. The original 246-ft bell-tower was demolished in 1931 because of fears it would topple; the replacement is 15 ft lower.

Across the street from Trinity on St James Avenue is the 740-ft ★ ★ ★ **New John Hancock Tower ⓱**, which had its own architectural problems while under construction in the early 1970s. The dramatic design by I. M. Pei and Partners called for more than 10,000 panes of reflec-

Towering over Trinity

tive glass to sheath an irregularly shaped, 60-story tower. Unanticipated stresses, however, caused the window glass to buckle and snap. Today, the tower is Boston's tallest building. The ★ ★ ★ **rooftop observatory** is a must stop for visitors. The 'old' John Hancock Tower, built in 1947, is much-loved for a stylish weather beacon which may be decoded according to a bit doggerel: 'Steady blue, clear view; flashing blue, clouds due; steady red, rain ahead; flashing red, snow ahead.' (In summer, flashing red indicates the day's Red Sox home game has been cancelled.)

If the weather is less than perfect – a not uncommon occurrence – the shopping malls of **Copley Place** and **Prudential Center** ('the Pru' to residents) make a hospitable retreat. Both complexes are somewhat out of character with their surroundings, more suburban than urban. In 1965 when it opened, the 50-story Prudential tower by Charles Luckman and Associates heralded a new, modern Boston, but its architectural vision of an antiseptic future quickly dimmed. In the early 1990s, after much public discussion, the cold and windswept complex was enclosed and reincarnated. The transformation was capped, literally and figuratively, in 1995 with a $4 million renovation of the **Top of the Hub** restaurant on the 52nd floor (tel: 536-1775) and **Skywalk** observatory on the 50th floor. The renovation project linked the Pru by glass bridges with neighboring Copley Place as well as the Hynes Convention Center. More than 100 stores and restaurants as well as three hotels are gathered here.

38

The Pru's exit at Huntington Avenue leads to the ★ **Christian Science Center**, 175 Huntington Avenue (tel. 450-2000), a sprawling complex that houses the international headquarters of the Church of Christ, Scientist. In 1875, Mary Baker Eddy published *Science and Health with Key to the Scriptures*, in which she outlined her philosophy of Christian Science and sought to restore, as she put it, 'primitive Christianity and its lost element of healing.' While ill herself, Eddy had read a New Testament account of healing by Jesus and was cured. The experience led her to believe that all disease was a product of the mind. Prayer acquired curative powers.

Christian Science Center

In 1892, the Church of Christ, Scientist was formally established in Boston, and the Christian Science Publishing Society began publishing the *Christian Science Monitor* newspaper in 1908. **The Mother Church** is actually two structures, the first built in 1893–94, and the 'Extension,' with its prominent dome, completed in 1906. Inside the Christian Science Publishing Society Building (1932) is the ★ **Mapparium**, a 30-ft diameter stained-glass globe of the earth bisected by a glass bridge. Around a long reflecting pool are three concrete-faced structures designed by I. M. Pei and Partners and completed in 1973.

Tour 5

Outdoor games

Harvard Square

On October 25, 1636, the same day it passed legislation forbidding the sale of lace for garments except for 'binding or small edging lace,' the Massachusetts General Court also 'agreed to give £400 towards a schoale or colledge' to be established at Newtowne on the north bank of the Charles River, 5 miles from Boston.

39

The Puritans' commitment to higher education in their fledgling settlement was hardly trifling, since £400 represented almost one-quarter of the Massachusetts Bay Colony's total tax levy that year. When you consider that the endowment of Harvard University today easily exceeds $6 billion, it's clear that the return on the Puritans' original investment reckoned in the advancement of learning is incalculable.

Sun and study

In September 1638, shortly after the college was opened, a 30-year-old clergyman of a well-to-do London family succumbed to consumption in Charlestown. On his deathbed, the Rev. John Harvard declared his wish to leave half his estate (about £1,700) and all his library to the college; the next spring, the General Court resolved to name the school in his honor as well as to change the name of Newtowne to Cambridge, after the English city where many Puritan leaders had been educated.

Harvard Square

Because parking is so limited around Harvard Square, the easiest way to get there is via the MBTA Red Line to Harvard station. Escalators and stair emerge from underground onto the center stage of Harvard Square, where Massachusetts Avenue, JFK Drive, and Brattle Street merge. An information kiosk operated by **Cambridge Discovery** (tel: 497-1630) provides maps and brochures and is located at the head of the stairs. Beside the 'T' station

Massachusetts Hall

The 'statue of three lies'

entrance is **Out of Town News** (tel: 354-7777), with a wide collection of national and international newspapers and magazines. The **Harvard Cooperative Society**, known familiarly as 'the Coop' (pronounced like chicken coop) stands across the street at 1400 Massachusetts Avenue (tel: 499-2000) and has a full line of souvenirs and clothing emblazoned with the Harvard University crest.

Johnston Gate, the main entrance to **Harvard Yard**, is 100 yards west on Massachusetts Avenue from the 'T' station. **Massachusetts Hall** (1720), to the right, is the oldest surviving college building and houses the office of the college president. To the left, **Harvard Hall** is the third structure of that name, and was built in 1764 after a fire consumed what was then the largest library in America, including books bequeathed by John Harvard.

Designed by Charles Bulfinch in 1813, the granite-faced **University Hall** lies across the lawn of the 'Old Yard' behind the 1884 ★ ★ ★ statue of **John Harvard** by Daniel Chester French. It is known whimsically as 'the statue of three lies' because (1) the figure is not John Harvard – no likeness of him is known to exist – but Sherman Hoar, a member of the Class of 1882; (2) John Harvard did not found the college, but was its first important benefactor; and (3) the college was established not in 1638, the year of Harvard's death, but two years earlier.

Continuing further in Harvard Yard, the Tercentary

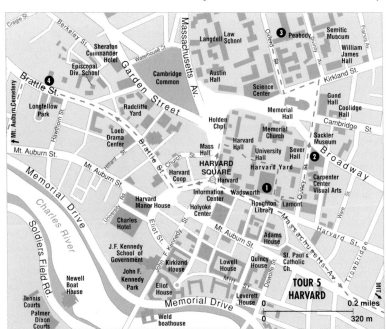

TOUR 5
HARVARD

Quadrangle or so-called 'New Yard' beyond University Hall is the site of the school's annual commencement activities. The white steeple of **Memorial Church**, built in 1931 to honor Harvard students and alumni killed in World War I, should look familiar – the model was the spire of Old North Church. The quadrangle's dominant structure is the 12-columned portico of the ★ ★ ★ **Widener Memorial Library ❶**, named for Harry Elkins Widener, a member of the Class of 1907 who went down with the *Titanic* in 1912. Harvard's vast book collection – exceeded in the US only by the Library of Congress and the New York Public Library – includes a 1623 First Folio of Shakespeare's plays as well as a Gutenberg bible, which are displayed in the **Widener Memorial Room**. In the adjacent **Houghton Library**, a display of rare books includes the only surviving volume from John Harvard's library.

Waiting at the Widener

Follow a footpath at the bottom of the Widener Library stairs roughly east to Quincy Street. Immediately striking by its stark appearance is the **Carpenter Center for the Visual Arts** (1961), 24 Quincy Street, the only US building by Le Corbusier. In a basement theater of the austere concrete structure, the **Harvard Film Archive** (tel: 495-4700) presents films from around the world.

41

★ ★ **William Hayes Fogg Art Museum ❷**, 32 Quincy Street (tel: 495-9400), is the oldest of Harvard's nine museums. It opened in 1895 and covers American and European painting and sculpture as well as housing temporary exhibitions. The Fogg's current home was completed in 1927; a handsome replica of an Italian loggia lies behind an unassuming neo-Georgian facade. A single Harvard art museums admission also allows entrance to the galleries of Central and Northern European art in the **Busch-Reisinger Museum** (tel: 495-9400), which may be entered through the Fogg, as well as the nearby **Arthur M. Sackler Museum**, 485 Broadway (tel: 495-9400), which features ancient Egyptian, Greek and Roman works as well as Chinese, Japanese and Islamic art.

Fogg Gallery finery

Sackler Museum

Turn right on Quincy Street and again cross Cambridge Street. On the left is **Memorial Hall**, begun in 1870 to honor Harvard's Civil War dead; its auditorium, Sanders Theater, hosts lectures and music concerts. To the right is the library and studios of **Graham Gund Hall** (1969), home of the Graduate School of Design.

Turn left at Kirkland Street, then right on Oxford Street, leading to the sprawling complex, on the right, of the ★ ★ **Harvard University Museums of Cultural and Natural History ❸** (for a map and information, tel: 495-3045), which Louis Agassiz ambitiously dedicated to 'the study of Earth and life on Earth.' Of the 100,000-plus works of art in the various museums, the **Ware Collection of Glass Flowers,** on the third floor of the ★ ★ ★ **Botanical**

Museum, is the most popular. Other highlights include Native American cultural artifacts at the **Peabody Museum of Archaeology and Ethnology**; the world's largest-known turtle shell in the **Museum of Comparative Zoölogy**; meteorites and a 3040-carat topaz gem in the **Mineralogical and Geological Museum**; and photography from the Middle East in the **Semitic Museum**.

Return to the Harvard Square 'T' station and cross to Brattle Street, which follows along the side and annex of the Coop department store, then turns sharply to the right opposite the HMV music store. The Cambridge Center for Adult Education has its headquarters in the **William Brattle House**, 42 Brattle Street, built in 1727 by the town's wealthiest citizen. Longfellow's poem *The Village Blacksmith* honored Dexter Pratt, his neighbor and the original owner of 56 Brattle Street, constructed in 1808 and now the **Blacksmith House Bakery & Cafe** (tel: 876-2725). The 'spreading chestnut' was cut down in 1876, despite protests from the Cambridge bard. The **Loeb Drama Center**, 64 Brattle Street, stages performances of classics and contemporary works by the American Repertory Theater throughout the year. **Radcliffe Yard**, of the women's college of the same name, lies opposite.

At the corner of Ash Street, the **Stoughton House**, 90 Brattle Street (not open to the public), was built in 1883 by Henry Hobson Richardson, architect of Copley Square's Trinity Church, and ranks as one of the first and most successful examples of the Shingle Style (the house was renovated and enlarged in 1900 by Richardson's successor firm).

Henry Wadsworth Longfellow, creator of Evangline and Hiawatha and myth-maker of Paul Revere's ride, lived at 105 Brattle Street from 1837 until his death in 1882. ★ ★ ★ **Longfellow National Historic Site ❹** (tel: 876-4491) preserves the belongings and the memory not only of Longfellow, but also of another famous resident, General George Washington, who made his headquarters there in 1775 and 1776 after taking command of the Continental Army. In the study, for example, are both the Chippendale chair where Washington sat while forming strategy with his staff, and a folding desk where Longfellow wrote. An elaborate flower garden at the estate was begun by Longfellow in 1845. Across the street, **Longfellow Park** includes a memorial sculpture by Daniel Chester French and the home Longfellow built for his son in 1870.

Leaving Longfellow Park, continue on Brattle Street a short distance to Willard Street, turn left toward the Charles River, then right on Mt Auburn Street. A 15-minute walk, crossing busy Rte 2, leads to ★ ★ **Mt Auburn Cemetery**, the nation's first garden cemetery, which opened in 1831 (the graveyard may be better and more

Forging ahead with lunch

Radcliffe Yard

Remembering Longfellow

quickly reached by a 'trackless trolley' bus from Harvard Square station, route 71). Final resting place of Longfellow, Bulfinch, Winslow Homer, Mary Baker Eddy, and many other distinguished Massachusetts natives, Mt Auburn Cemetery may be appreciated for the ornate architecture of its tombs as well as for the splendor of its plantings. The silence and calm of this urban oasis further attracts a wide range of migratory birds.

Mt Auburn Cemetery

Return again to Harvard Square. At an MBTA bus stop on Massachusetts Avenue in front of the yellow-clapboard **Wadsworth House**, which was General Washington's headquarters before he moved to 105 Brattle Street, take the route no. 1 bus (marked, 'Dudley') about 1½ miles along Massachusetts Avenue to the **Massachusetts Institute of Technology**. Founded in Boston in 1861, MIT moved from Copley Square to the banks of the Charles River in Cambridge in 1916. Scientists working at the school's Servomechanisms Lab developed 'Whirlwind,' the grandfather of digital computers, which when completed in 1951 filled several large rooms.

Rogers Building, MIT

On the East Campus, the granite-domed ★ ★ **Rogers Building**, 77 Massachusetts Avenue, is known to MIT students as 'Lobby 7.' An MIT information office inside (tel: 253-4795) offers free maps and guided campus tours. The bare lobby is representative of the entire labyrinthine complex, linked by factory-like corridors. Immediately accessible from the Rogers Building (named for geologist William Barton Rogers, the school's founder and first president) is the **Francis Russell Hart Nautical Museum**, which displays ships' models, and the **Margaret Hutchinson Compton Gallery**, which presents exhibits of items from the MIT historical collection.

Moore masterpieces

Directly across from the main entrance to Lobby 7, follow what students call 'the infinite corridor' through several buildings to an exit onto Killian Court where Henry Moore's rotund masterpiece, *Three-Piece Reclining Figure, Draped* (1973) is surrounded by the trim, classical forms of the Maclaurin Buildings. **Hayden Memorial Library**, 160 Memorial Drive, displays art and sculpture.

Across Massachusetts Avenue on MIT's West Campus, **Kresge Auditorium** (rear of 48 Massachusetts Avenue) is the most prominent feature: a carapace of glass and steel with a wood-paneled interior, Kresge was designed in 1954 by the Finnish architect Eero Saarinen, who also is responsible for the brick cylinder of the nearby windowless **MIT Chapel**. A half-mile from the center of MIT's campus, the **MIT Museum**, 265 Massachusetts Avenue (tel: 253-4444), featuring scientific instruments and documents on the school's history. The **MIT List Visual Art Center**, 20 Ames Street (tel: 253-4680), devoted to contemporary art in all media, is on the East Campus.

Kresge Auditorium

Memorial Day march, Concord

Excursion 1

Lexington and Concord

A Redcoat haunt

Battle Green memorial

On Saturday, April 17, 1775, Paul Revere and others in Boston observed an alarming trend in British troop movements. Redcoats of the 29th Regiment had been stationed at the Common since 1768, and they were watched closely by resident patriots. Unexpectedly, routine patrols were cancelled and work was begun to ready troop boats for action. Bostonians surmised that the British were preparing either to arrest John Hancock and Samuel Adams, who were in Lexington for a meeting of the Massachusetts Provincial Congress, or else to seize a cache of arms hidden in nearby Concord. Revere, principal rider for the Boston Committee of Safety, rode out the next morning to warn them, then returned to Boston. He would make the same journey again that night – with momentous effect.

The clash of British troops and Massachusetts 'Minutemen' on April 19, 1775, pitted Goliath against David – with a similar result. First on the Lexington Green, then at the North Bridge across the Concord River, the pressure cooker that were the 13 colonies boiled over. In Lexington, Captain Parker told his men: 'Stand your ground, don't fire unless fired upon, but if they mean to have a war, let it begin here!' And so it did. By day's end, after nearly 40 miles of marching, the Redcoats returned to Boston, leaving a bloody chain of dead and wounded on both sides.

Lexington, 12 miles west of Boston, may be reached by Massachusetts Avenue from Cambridge or from Route 2. MBTA buses travel to Lexington Center from the Alewife Red Line station and MBTA commuter rail trains stop in Concord on the Fitchburg line from North Station as well as the Red Line's Porter Square Station.

At the Junction of Massachusetts Avenue and Route 2A, just outside historic Lexington, is the ★ **Museum of Our National Heritage**, 33 Marrett Road, Lexington (tel: 861-6559). Founded in 1976 as a Bicentennial gift by the Scottish Rite of Freemasonry, the museum presents changing exhibits on American history and popular culture as well as *Lexington Alarm'd*, a permanent show detailing the opening of the American Revolutionary War.

While the owner and his family hid in nearby woods, British redcoats arriving from Boston made a temporary HQ on April 19, 1775 at the **Munroe Tavern**, 1332 Massachusetts Avenue (tel: 674-9238). As they retreated later in the day, the Redcoats left their wounded here.

A mile farther on Massachusetts Avenue is ★ ★ **Battle Green,** perhaps the country's most famous 2-acre plot. The prominent **Minuteman Statue**, by Henry Hudson Kitson depicting a Yankee farmer with musket, commemorates the unassuming heroes of the day. Captain Parker's famous command to his men is inscribed to the right of the Minuteman's statue. The town's helpful **Visitors Center**, run by the Lexington Chamber of Commerce, is at 1875 Massachusetts Avenue (tel: 862-1450).

The Minuteman Statue

When the Minutemen assembled at dawn, they were not sure how to greet the British. Several of those under command of Captain John Parker hadn't even bothered to bring ammunition. No one knows who fired the first shot. At colorful battle recreations held here on the third Monday of April, gunfire commences simultaneously.

Wounded Minutemen were carried inside ★ **Buckman Tavern**, One Bedford Street (tel: 862-5598), on the east side of Battle Green. By the door are holes where wayward Redcoat musket balls struck. Inside is the tavern's original 17th-century furniture and cooking equipment. Altogether, eight Massachusetts men were killed and 10 wounded. Struck by a musket ball, Captain Parker was finished off with a Redcoat bayonet thrust. The Americans had fired disorderly and only one British soldier received a flesh wound.

Buckman Tavern

A short stroll up Hancock Street leads to the **Hancock-Clarke House**, 36 Hancock Street (tel: 861-0928). When unsuspecting Redcoats released Paul Revere shortly after his famous ride, he scurried here to warn fellow patriots Samuel Adams and John Hancock. Revere was able to see the pair off before British troops arrived at Lexington Green for the fateful confrontation with the Minutemen. As they sped away in a carriage heading in the opposite direction, the feisty Adams remarked about the glorious morning. Hancock, a well-to-do dandy, thought his companion referred to the weather. 'I mean,' said Adams patiently, 'what a glorious morning for America.'

A freed man remembered

Traveling west on Route 2A traces what is left of the

Battle Road Visitors Center
Orchard House

'**Battle Road**,' along which the confident British marched toward Concord to the music of fife and drum. The 750-acre **Minute Man National Historic Park** is on the left. One mile from Lexington on the right is ★ ★ ★ **Battle Road Visitors Center**, off Route 2A (tel: 862-7753), considered the best place for historical information.

Arranged in a row on the right of Route 2A (Lexington Road) are three historic houses associated with 19th-century Concord, when the New England village was a kind of Athens in miniature, a literary and philosophical hotbed. Here Ralph Waldo Emerson, the Transcendentalist philosopher, composed his essays and provided occasional meals to his friend and neighbor Henry David Thoreau when he was living at Walden Pond.

Also Concord residents at one time or another were the likes of novelist Nathaniel Hawthorne, poet William Ellery Channing, and education reformer and famous father Amos Bronson Alcott. At ★ ★ **Orchard House**, 399 Lexington Road (tel: 508-369-4118), the Alcott family lived from 1858 to 1877, and here Louisa May Alcott wrote *Little Women*. At **The Wayside**, 455 Lexington Road (tel: 508-369-6975), Nathaniel Hawthorne, lived from 1852 until his death in 1864. Next door, the **Grapevine Cottage**, 491 Lexington Road (not open to public), displays a plaque that details how in 1843, Ephraim Wales Bull first sowed the Concord grape at his nearby farm.

At the junction of Route 2A and the Cambridge Turnpike, the ★ ★ **Concord Antiquarian Museum**, 200 Lexington Road, tel: 508-369-9609) has 17 rooms of antiques, including a lantern purported to have hung beside another in Old North Church as a signal to Paul Revere. Because of fear of fire, Emerson's Study was transferred here from the nearby wooden Emerson House. In the Thoreau Room is the bed where the back-to-nature essayist slept at Walden Pond; the museum boasts the world's largest collection of Thoreau artifacts. Across the road, **Ralph Waldo Emerson House**, 28 Cambridge Turnpike, on Route 2A (tel: 508-369-2236) has books from his library as well as the writer's own furnishings.

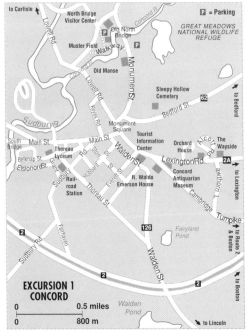

EXCURSION 1
CONCORD

0   0.5 miles
0   800 m

A 15-minute walk reaches the center of Concord, whose Chamber of Commerce has a **tourist information center** at Heywood Street, (tel: 508-369-3120). **Monument Square** has a memorial to Civil War dead. The **Colonial Inn**, 48 Monument Square (tel: 508-369-9200) serves hearty meals, as it has since before the Revolution. The town has many attractive boutiques as well as the generously stocked **Concord Bookshop** at 65 Main Street.

Parading the past

Concord's prominent permanent population resides at ★★ **Sleepy Hollow Cemetery**, a short stroll from the Inn along Bedford Street. In the northeast corner at **Author's Ridge**, rest the Alcotts (Louisa May and her father, who died two days apart in 1888, shared the same birthday and the same funeral), along with Hawthorne, Thoreau and Emerson. A bronze table on Emerson's quartz stone grave marker declares: 'The passive master lent his hand/To the vast soul o'er which him planned.' Less lofty are the sentiments engraved over Ephraim Wales Bull's final resting place – 'He sowed, others reaped' (the developer of the Concord grape had failed to profit from his work).

Old Manse

Return to Monument Square and once again, pick up the trail of Redcoats and Minuteman along Monument Street, passing the **Old Manse** (tel: 508-369-3909), built in 1770 for the Rev. William Emerson, and later occupied by Ralph Waldo Emerson and Nathaniel Hawthorne. Enter the ★★★ **National Historic Park** and cross a contemporary reconstruction of the famous 'rude bridge.' On the other side of 'Old North Bridge' waits the Minuteman statue by Concord resident Daniel Chester French. Further information can be found at **North Bridge Visitor Center**, 174 Liberty Street (tel: 508-369-6993).

Old North Bridge

At North Bridge, Major John Pitcairn and his men crossed the Concord River to take the house of Colonel James Barrett, where American arms were supposedly stockpiled. When fire began in the town courthouse and elsewhere, Concord's defenders let fly with 'the shot heard 'round the world.' The element of surprise was in the Massachusetts men's favor, and the Redcoats took their first serious casualties, including three dead. In short order, the British began a disorderly retreat to Boston.

In summer, the crowd of bathers at ★★★ **Walden Pond** (tel: 508-369-3254), a 10-minute walk from the intersection of Routes 2 and 126, overwhelms any search for the quiet solitude Thoreau sought there. The decision to build a cabin in 1845 at Emerson's estate at Walden Pond came upon Henry David Thoreau after a dozen years of 'pursuing my intuition.' He declared his intention plainly: 'I went to the woods because I wished to live deliberately, to front only the essential facts of life, and see if I could not learn what it had to teach, and not, when I came to die, discover that I had not lived.'

Walden Pond

Excursion 2

Salem

Every witch way

Curiously for a city that's a by-word for hysterical intolerance, Salem takes its name from *shalom*, the Hebrew word for 'peace.' Today, of course, Salem is an attractive and richly historical waterfront city 20 miles north of Boston that is decidedly peaceful. At its defining moment in 1692, however, the air here and in surrounding settlements was charged with fear and recrimination.

In January 1692, several young women, including the daughter and niece of minister Samuel Parris, began to exhibit strange and inexplicable behavior at their home in Salem Village (now called Danvers). Their symptoms included blasphemous screaming, convulsive seizures, trance-like states and mysterious 'spells.'

Pressed to identify the source of their torments, the girls denounced Tituba, a slave in the Parris household who was born in Barbados and may have told the girls provocative Caribbean tales, along with two local women, Sarah Osborne, a widow of some property who enjoyed male company and did not regularly attend church services, and the destitute and slovenly Sarah Good. Tituba's 'confession' – she claimed to have conversed with winged cats and red rats – persuaded officials that demonic possession was rife in their midst. In the ensuing 'witch hunt' 27 townspeople were convicted, 19 were hanged and four died in

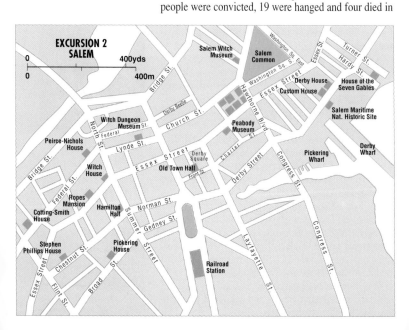

EXCURSION 2 SALEM

0 — 400yds
0 — 400m

Bridge St.
Salem Witch Museum
Salem Common
Washington Sq. East
Essex St.
Turner St.
Hardy St.
Washington Sq. S
Essex Street
Derby House
Custom House
House of the Seven Gables
Derby Beabe
Church St.
North St.
Witch Dungeon Museum
Federal St.
Hawthorne Blvd
Peabody Museum
Salem Maritime Nat. Historic Site
Peirce-Nichols House
Lynde St.
Essex Street
Derby Square
Old Town Hall
Charter
Derby Street
Pickering Wharf
Derby Wharf
Bridge St.
Witch House
Front St.
Congress St.
Federal St.
Ropes Mansion
Norman St.
Hamilton Hall
Cotting-Smith House
Summer Street
Gedney St.
Stephen Phillips House
Chestnut St.
Pickering House
Lafayette St.
Congress St.
Essex Street
Flint St.
Broad St.
Railroad Station

Hanging around at the Witch Museum

jail. The tide finally turned when a Boston merchant complained to Governor William Phips, who dissolved the special court session in October.

An astonishing maritime legacy also draws visitors. Following the Revolutionary War, Salem thrived in the new China Trade and became one of the world's busiest ports, if only briefly. When they had the opportunity, Salem's canny captains cornered the world market on black pepper, tea, spices and silk. The wealth they made in the Orient was used in Salem to build fabulous mansions.

49

Salem's attractions make for an active and rewarding day trip, and its compact area make it possible to tour almost entirely by foot. It is easily reached on the MBTA Rockport commuter rail line from North Station. A self-guided **Heritage Trail** snakes through the city for slightly under 2 miles and connects all major sites. **National Park Service Visitor Center**, 2 Liberty Street (tel: 508-740-1650) provides maps and information as well as presenting films and exhibits. **Salem Trolley Corp.**, 9 Pickering Way, (tel: 508-7444 5469) departs from here regularly and stops at over a dozen attractions.

Salem's selling point

Peabody Essex Museum

Everyone's first stop in 'the Witch City' is naturally the ★ ★ ★ **Witch Museum**, Washington Square (tel: 508-744-1692). Inside the turreted Romanesque castle are 13 (coincidence? think again!) stage sets with life-size models plus a gripping audio-visual presentation.

Surrounding the Visitor Center, in a multi-building complex, is the ★ ★ ★ **Peabody Essex Museum**, East India Square, Salem (tel: 508-745-9500). The Peabody Museum of Salem, founded in 1799 by mariners and merchants of the East India Marine Society, is the nation's oldest continuously operating museum; in 1992, it merged with the Essex Institute, a historical society founded in 1821. The combined collections feature nearly half a million objects in 30 galleries of permanent and changing exhibitions.

Salem Witch Village and New England Pirate Museum

Derby Wharf

One block south on Liberty Street at the corner of Charter Street is the ★ **Witch Trials Memorial**. Dedicated in 1992, the trial's tricentennial, the design inspires reflection on human rights and tolerance. Behind is the **Old Burying Point**, Salem's oldest burying ground (1637).

At the corner of Charter Street and Derby Street is the new **Wax Museum of Witches and Seafarers**, 288 Derby Street (tel: 508-740-2929), which opened in 1993. Directly opposite is ★ ★ **Salem Witch Village**, 282 Rear Derby Street (tel: 508-740-9229), where visitors can explore myths and facts about witchcraft through the ages.

Before they became obsessed with witches, Salem's merchants hired Captain Kidd in 1691 to hunt down the hated Blackbeard. When he failed to capture the scourge of New England's high seas, Kidd turned to piracy himself. Swashbuckling stories are told at the **New England Pirate Museum**, 274 Derby Street (tel: 508-741-2800).

Continuing eastward on Derby Street brings you to ★ ★ ★ **Pickering Wharf** (information, tel: 508-745-9540), a harborside marketplace of boutiques and restaurants. Directly adjacent is the ★ ★ ★ **Salem Maritime National Historic Site**, 174 Derby Street (tel: 508-740-1680). Guided tours cover various maritime buildings of the 9-acre **Derby Wharf** and the nearby 1819 ★ ★ **Custom House**, where Nathaniel Hawthorne once worked.

Return to Derby Street, continue east and turn right at Hardy Street. By the harbor's edge lies the ★ ★ ★ **House of the Seven Gables**, 54 Turner Street (tel: 508-744-0991). Guides in Edwardian costume welcome visitors to the 'rusty wooden house with seven acutely peaked gables,' a 1668 mansion that supposedly inspired Hawthorne's romantic novel, as well as to the novelist's own birthplace nearby and several other 17th-century dwellings.

Pick up the Heritage Trail again at the corner of Hardy and Essex streets and stroll west to the ★ ★ **Witch House**, 310 Essex Street (tel: 508-744-0180). The restored home of witch trial Judge Jonathan Corwin, this is the only structure still standing with direct ties to the 1692 events.

Architecture aficionados will want to make time for a walk along Salem's ★ ★ ★ **Chestnut Street**, designated a National Historic Landmark for its superb collection of Federal Era townhouses. The Peabody Essex Museum maintains three important houses in the area, including the ★ ★ **Ropes Mansion** on Essex Street.

In Forest River Park, at the junction of Route 1A and Route 129 is ★ ★ **Salem 1630: Pioneer Village** (tel: 508-745-0525), a re-created 17th-century New England fishing village. The 5-acre site includes wigwams, thatched roof cottages, sheep and goats grazing in a meadow, and a blacksmith at work. The site, about 3 miles from Salem's center, is accessible by public bus.

Excursion 3

Gloucester

Of all areas in Massachusetts settled by English colonists, only Plymouth has a longer history than **Cape Ann**. In 1623, the Dorchester Company under Roger Conant established a fishing post at what is now Gloucester. The first hardy English fishermen have long since been supplanted by equally hardy Italians and Portuguese. Sadly, overfishing of once plentiful stock of cod and ground fish has endangered their livelihood. Its commercial link with the sea may be loosening, but Cape Ann has not lost hold on those seeking contact with the water found at the end of a pier lined with restaurants and art galleries.

En route to Gloucester on Route 127, visitors pass through the town's well-to-do Magnolia section. An imposing presence set above rocky shores, the ★ ★ ★ **Hammond Castle Museum**, 80 Hesperus Avenue (tel: 508-283-2080), was a showcase for inventor John Hays Hammond, Jr's eclectic collection of European art objects. A 'reanimation' of slices of life from Romanesque, Medieval and Renaissance Italy, France and Spain, the central courtyard opens onto a mini-town square with 15th-century French house facades.

'Man at the Wheel'

51

In 1623, Gloucester's first settlers arrived at Fishermen's Field, near what is now **Betty Smith Park** and **Stage Fort Park**, overlooking Gloucester Harbor on Stacy Boulevard near the fisherman's statue. **The Gloucester Visitors Welcoming Center** is also at the site.

★ ★ ★ '**Man at the Wheel**,' depicting a wind-lashed sailor and inscribed to 'They that Go down to the Sea in Ships,' stands as a gateway to Gloucester on Stacy Boulevard (Route 127). The trademark sculpture was commissioned in 1923 and created locally by Leonard Craske.

Cape Ann Chamber of Commerce, 33 Commercial Street (tel: 508-283-1601/1-800-321-0133) provides maps and information, including a map and guide to the **Gloucester Maritime Trail**, four self-guided walking tours highlighting distinctive portions of the waterfront. Otherwise, **Salt Water Trolleys** (tel: 508-283-7916) travel to major attractions and beaches on Cape Ann on Saturdays, Sundays and holidays from June to mid-September.

The Downtown Loop, a 1-mile walking trail, begins at **St Peter's Park**, named for the patron saint of fishermen. Turn right at the Harbor Loop, and continue past the US Coast Guard Station, a working military base, closed to the public. In summer, the ★ ★ **Schooner** *Adventure* (tel: 508-281-8079) a National Historic Landmark, is docked not far away (open to visitors in summer from Thursday to Sunday; *Adventure*'s winter berth is at

Jodrey State Fish Pier). Built of oak and pine in nearby Essex, the 121-ft schooner spent 27 years fishing the North Atlantic's outer banks from Gloucester and Boston.

Cross through a parking lot and climb a set of stairs beside the Police Station to Main Street, turn left, then right to Pleasant Street. ★ ★ ★ **Cape Ann Historical Museum**, Cape Ann Historical Association, 27 Pleasant Street, at the corner of Federal Street, (tel: 508-283-0455) exhibits the nation's largest collection of paintings and drawings by Fitz Hugh Lane (1804–65), one of America's most important 19th-century artists. The museum's Fisheries Maritime Galleries feature three historically significant vessels, including *Centennial*, the vessel Alfred Johnson used in the first single-handed crossing of the Atlantic.

Retrace Pleasant Street to Middle Street, which is lined with attractive late 18th-century homes. A 15-room Georgian mansion, the **Sargent-Murray-Gilman-Hough House**, 49 Middle Street (tel: 508-281-2432), is open for tours. At the corner of Middle Street and Church Street, the **Universalist Church**, erected in 1805, was the first of its kind in America and houses a Paul Revere bell.

Sargent-Murray-Gilman-Hough House

52

In East Gloucester, the **North Shore Art Association**, (197 East Main Street, tel: 508-283-1857) founded in 1923, is the oldest art association of its kind in the US. A large collection of paintings and sculpture is on show in a renovated wharf building overlooking Smith Cove. Turn right toward the water along Rocky Neck Avenue, home to art galleries and restaurants. Still more galleries and artists' studios are open at the ★ ★ **Rocky Neck Art Colony**, long a haven for the aspiring and the established.

Rocky Neck Art Colony

Continuing toward Eastern Point, ★ ★ ★ **Beauport, The Sleeper-McCann House**, 75 Eastern Point Blvd. (tel: 508-283-0800) overlooks Gloucester Harbor from the east. In 1907 by Henry Davis Sleeper, a prominent collector and interior designer, began the house's construction and evolved over nearly 30 years into a maze of 40 rooms filled with vast collections of American and European objects, all artfully arranged by Sleeper. Charles and Helena McCann bought Beauport after Sleeper's death and installed their own extensive collection of Chinese export porcelain, but otherwise preserved the house nearly intact.

The self-proclaimed '**Whale-Watching Capital of the World**,' Gloucester benefits from its proximity to the Stellwagen Banks (as a result, whale-watching trips taken from Gloucester last half as long as those leaving from Boston). Local operators include **Cape Ann Whale Watch** and the Whale Conversation Institute, Rose's Wharf (tel: 508-283-5110/1-800-877-5110); **Capt. Bill & Sons** and the Cetacean Research Unit, departs from Harbor Loop (tel: 508-283-6995/1-800-339-4253); **Yankee Whale Watch** and the Atlantic Cetacean Research Center, 75W Essex

Whale watchers

Avenue (tel: 508-283-0313/1-800-942-5464); **Seven Seas Whale Watch**, Seven Seas Wharf, Rogers Street (tel: 508-283-1776/1-800-238-1776).

At the tip of Cape Ann, **Rockport** ranks among America's most picturesque harbor towns. ★ ★ ★ **Motif #1**, on Bradley wharf, is a quaint clapboard sail loft decorated with buoys that is supposedly the most photographed and most painted building in the country. Bearskin Neck, a finger of land curling around the harbor and lined with shops and restaurants, ends at **Old Stone Fort**, a small stockade built by public subscription during the War of 1812.

Like Gloucester, Rockport has long served as an inspiring setting for artists enamored of the sea. ★ ★ **Rockport Art Association**, 12 Main Street (tel: 508-546-6604), has a fine exhibition of paintings, graphics and sculptures by local artists on local subjects. In 1814, the British man-of-war *Nymph* fired at the **Old Sloop Congregational Church**, Main Street, to silence its bell, which which had been rung to alarm the town. The shot landed in the tower support, however, where it can still be seen.

Motif # 1

At the opposite end of town is the **Hannah Jumper House** (corner of Mount Pleasant Street and Atlantic Avenue), whose namesake led the women of Rockport in the Hatchet Gang Raid, July 8, 1856, to rid the town of liquor. Rockport is still 'dry'. A rocky mount at the end of Atlantic Avenue, the **Headlands** offers spectacular views of the harbor, and attracts artists and picnickers.

Rockport harbor

Rockport's oddest attraction is the ★ ★ **Paper House** on Pigeon Hill Street, Pigeon Cove. Swedish immigrant Ellis Stenman, who read nine newspapers daily, fashioned his unique abode between 1922 and 1942 from 100,000 newspapers layered 215 thick, then rolled, glued and varnished. Unusual furnishings include a grandfather's clock made from newspapers of the capital cities of the then 48 states, and a writing desk made from stories about Col. Charles Lindbergh's historic trans-Atlantic flight.

A rural town of 3,000 on the northern flank of Cape Ann, **Essex** has 60 antique dealers and a dozen restaurants arranged along a scenic coastal stretch of Route 133.

As fishing is Gloucester, shipbuilding was to Essex, where 4,000 vessels were built, most in the 19th century. ★ ★ **Essex Shipbuilding Museum**, John Wise Avenue, (tel: 508-768-7541) features drawings, tools, photographs, rigged ship models and 15 builders' half-models on loan from Smithsonian, all displayed in an 1834 schoolhouse. Established in 1914, **Woodman's Lobster Pool**, 125 Main Street (tel: 508-768-6451), is the home of the fried clam, a New England favorite since its invention in 1916. The highlight of the **Essex Clamfest**, the town's annual tribute to the magnificent mussel held on the second Saturday in September, is a clam chowder tasting competition.

Museums and Libraries

Intellectual curiosity and good fortune in business stimulated Bostonians to seek out the best in the world of art, painting and literature as early as the 18th century. The legacy of such acquisitiveness is now displayed at the area's major museums and libraries. The Museum of Fine Arts, in particular, but also the Isabella Stewart Gardner Museum and the museum of Harvard University, have permanent collections of international stature.

Major Boston museums covered in other sections of this guide are the **Museum of Science**, **Children's Museum** and **Computer Museum** (*see page 76*); and the **Museum of Afro-American History** (*see page 33*).

Boston

Boston Tea Party Ship and Museum, Congress Street bridge (tel: 338-1773). The *Beaver II*, a replica of a British ship boarded by Bostonians in the tax revolt of 1773, is docked not far from the original site at Griffin's Wharf, now on dry land. Following a tour led by guides in colonial-era costume, complimentary 'tax-free' tea is served.

Tossing the tea

55

Institute of Contemporary Art, 955 Boylston Street (tel: 266-5152) shows work by emerging and established artists but has no permanent collection.

Isabella Stewart Gardner Museum, 280 The Fenway (tel: 566-1401) is an eclectic melange of architectural elements from Venetian window frames to Roman mosaic floor tiles purposefully assembled as a suitably rich setting for galleries crammed with 2,500 objects, most notably masterpieces of European painting by Raphael, Rembrandt and Titian as well as recent work by Degas, Matisse, and James McNeill Whistler. Isabella Stewart Gardner became a serious collector on her father's death in 1891 when she inherited, tax-free, $1.6 million – a sum equivalent to at least $160 million today. Renowned for her love of flowers, Mrs Gardner directed construction of an interior courtyard with a glass roof so that plants and flowers might thrive year-round. According to provisions in her own will, 'Fenway Court' (the name she gave to her home-cum-museum) appears today much as it did at her death. Nothing may be sold or added. In 1990, however, thieves masquerading as police removed an estimated $200 million worth of paintings, including *The Concert* by Jan Vermeer, that have never been recovered.

Isabella Stewart Gardner Museum

A native New Yorker of clearly extravagant means, Isabella Stewart married John Lowell Gardner of an equally wealthy Boston family in 1860. Until her death in 1924, 'Mrs Jack' cultivated a reputation for unconventional behavior in the primly conventional society of Victorian Boston. Although she apparently did not keep

Museum of Fine Arts

The collections are diverse

lions in her cellar or walk them on a leash down Beacon Street (as legend has it), Mrs Gardner had wide-ranging interests, from Oriental philosophy to the Boston Red Sox.

Fenway Court was opened for the first time on New Year's Night 1903 with a concert by members of the Boston Symphony Orchestra and Mrs Gardner engaged many private performances by Paderewski, Nellie Melba and Gerald and Sarah Murphy, who serenaded her with African-American folk songs. The Gardner Museum continues to present more than 125 concerts a year.

Mapparium, Christian Science Church Center, 175 Huntington Avenue (tel: 450-3790). Visitors enter a 30-ft diameter stained-glass globe marked with the now forgotten borders of a pre-World War II planet. Anyone remember the Belgian Congo?

Museum of Fine Arts, 465 Huntington Avenue (tel: 267-9300) has departments in Asiatic art, Egyptian art, classical art, European decorative arts and sculpture, American decorative arts and sculpture, paintings, drawings and photographs, textiles and costumes, and modern art. Together, the MFA's holdings make it one of the nation's most outstanding art museums. In addition, it regularly stages critically-acclaimed 'super shows.'

On the lawn in front of entrance to the original 1909 museum building by Guy Lowell is the MFA's trademark sculpture by Cyrus Dallin, *Appeal to the Great Spirit*, depicting a Plains Indian in feathered headdress with arms outstretched and eyes uplifted. The museum's bunker-like West Wing (entrance at Museum Road), was designed by I. M. Pei, and since its opening in 1981 is where most special exhibitions are hung.

The MFA's massive collection has something to please everyone and any abbreviated recitation necessarily will ignore numerous equally worthwhile selections. Nevertheless, visitors will want to seek out several highlights.

Boston's premier colonial portrait artist, John Singleton Copley, is represented by dozens of excellent pieces, notably life-like portraits of the patriots Samuel Adams and Paul Revere. The latter's own exquisite work in silver is well-represented in the museum. Major New England artists frequently depicted local subjects, among such works are *Boston Harbor* by Fitz Hugh Lane, *Fog Warning* by Winslow Homer, and *Boston Common at Twilight* by Frederick Childe Hassam.

One of the largest collections anywhere of art from Japan and China, the Asiatic Department spans from Chinese ceramics of the 6th century to 18th-century Japanese scrolls depicting *The Gay Quarters of Kyoto*. These were chiefly amassed in the 19th century by local collectors while on trade voyages to the Far East in clipper ships.

The Egyptian rooms have mummies, statues, jewelry

and funereal objects dating to the Old Kingdom (2778–2360 BCE). A 'pair statue' depicting King Mycerinus and Queen Kha-Merer-Nebty is the oldest known of its kind.

Face from the Fine Arts

Throughout the 19th century, Boston collectors gravitated to works by French painters and were among the first anywhere to adopt the Impressionists. Major works by Degas, Delacroix, Gauguin, Millet, Monet, Manet, Pissaro and Renoir are among the most popular.

A fascinating series of rooms in the American Decorative Arts department display period furniture and furnishings from the Karolik collection. Also notable is a superior antique musical instrument collection.

Cambridge
For information on museums at Harvard University and Massachusetts Institute of Technology, see pages 41–43.

Libraries

Boston Athenaeum, 10½ Beacon Street (tel: 227-0270) is a private library, one of the nation's oldest, whose vast holdings include most of George Washington's own library. Free guided tours by appointment on Tuesdays and Thursdays, 3pm (book one day ahead).

57

Boston Public Library, 666 Boylston Street (tel: 536-5400), the first free city library supported by taxes, is actually two buildings: an ornate 1895 structure in the Italian Renaissance style by McKim, Mead and White; and an austere 1972 addition by Philip Johnson. Recent renovations at the older building have reinvigorated its opulent interior spaces with murals by Sargent, Abbey, and de Chavannes and sculpture by French and Saint-Gaudens.

Boston Public Library

French Library and Cultural Center, 53 Marlborough Street (tel: 266-4351) is Boston's own bibliothèque/mediathèque for the Francophone and Francophile. Back Bay neighbor, **Goethe Institut-German Cultural Center**, 170 Beacon Street (tel: 262-6050) promotes German culture, including literature and film.

John Fitzgerald Kennedy Library, Columbia Point (tel: 929-4523), housed in an I. M. Pei's white concrete tower and smoked-glass pavilion, is dedicated to the memory of the 35th President. Rededicated in 1993, the 'new' museum provides a 'you are there' experience with re-created settings from the Kennedy presidency including a television studio, site of the first presidential TV debate, and the Oval Office, as well as 20 video presentations on the Cuban Missile Crisis, the Civil Rights movement, and the assassination aftermath.

Meeting up at the Widener

Harry Elkins Widener Memorial Library, Harvard Yard, Cambridge (tel: 495-2411), is the principal library of Harvard College and was named for a member of the Class of 1907 lost with the *Titanic* (see page 41).

Concert at the Hatch Shell

Theater and Music

For its range of cultural venues, Boston has few equals in the United States. Local audiences support a weighty number of groups devoted to all the major arts. Over time, Boston's stages, concert halls and music clubs have nurtured artists of the highest caliber.

The Boston Symphony Orchestra under the direction of Seiji Ozawa is a longstanding critical and popular success. The Pulitzer Prize-winning playwright August Wilson regularly brings his dramas of African-American life to the Huntington Theatre before taking them to Broadway. At the American Repertory Theatre, the Tony-winning actress Cherry Jones was for many years a company member. Choreographer Mark Morris cultivated his talents at the Dance Umbrella and still returns regularly to Boston.

Back Bay buskers
Music lovers

Bostix, situated in Faneuil Hall Marketplace and Copley Square (tel: 482-2849) is Boston's official arts and entertainment kiosk providing tickets, including half-price day-of-show tickets, for theater, music, dance, museums, and other local attractions.

Classical music

Boston Lyric Opera, 114 State Street (tel: 248-8811) stages three productions annually. **Boston Symphony Orchestra**, Symphony Hall, 301 Massachusetts Avenue (tel: 266-1492) performs October–April. It moves to Tanglewood (in Lenox) for the summer, making way for the **Boston Pops** to play light musical fare from mid-May through mid-July (in addition to performances at Symphony Hall, the Pops play a series of free concerts, most notably a Fourth of July extravaganza complete with fireworks, at the Hatch Shell on the Charles River Esplanade). **Boston Philharmonic** performs at Jordan Hall, 30 Gainsborough Street (tel: 868-6696).

Handel & Haydn Society, 300 Massachusetts Avenue (tel: 266-3605), is the nation's oldest continuously performing arts group; it presented its first concert on Christmas Day 1815 and has played Handel's *Messiah* annually since 1854. **Longy School of Music**, One Follen Street, Cambridge (tel: 876-0956) has an active concert schedule year-round. **New England Conservatory of Music**, 30 Gainsborough Street (tel: 262-1120) presents lectures, seminars and 450 free classical, jazz and improvisation music concerts each year at Jordan Hall.

Dance

Ballet Theatre of Boston, 186 Massachusetts Avenue (tel: 262-0961), brings contemporary works to the Emerson Majestic Theatre. **Boston Ballet**, 19 Clarendon Street (tel: 695-6950), presents a glittery *Nutcracker* at Christmas as well as classical and contemporary programs. **Dance Umbrella**, 380 Green Street, Cambridge (tel: 492-7578) has earned a national reputation.

Theaters & Drama Companies

American Repertory Theatre, 64 Brattle Street, Cambridge (tel: 495-2668) for original plays and originally restaged classics. **Colonial Theatre**, 106 Boylston Street (tel: 426-9366) presenting major Broadway shows. **Emerson Majestic Theatre**, 219 Tremont Street (tel: 578-8727) was recently restored by new owners Emerson College.

Gloucester Stage Company, 2647 E. Main Street, Gloucester, is led by artistic director and playwright Israel Horowitz. **Huntington Theatre Company**, 264 Huntington Avenue (tel: 266-0800) stages both classic and contemporary plays September–June. **Lyric Stage**, 140 Clarendon Street (tel: 437-7172) produces new plays and classics including the perennial favorite *A Child's Christmas in Wales.*

At the **Charles Playhouse**, 74 Warrenton Street (tel: 451-0195), *Shear Madness*, a comedy whodunit with local references, is America's longest-running play. **Schubert Theatre**, 265 Tremont Street (tel: 482-9393) is a prominent venue for Broadway try-outs.

Wang Center for the Performing Arts, 268 Tremont Street (tel: 482-9393) is an elegantly restored movie palace, and is now home to major theatre, music and dance performances. **Wheelock Family Theatre**, Wheelock College, 180 The Riverway (tel: 734-5203) caters for a young audience.

59

Coming attractions

Drama at Quincy Market

Food and Drink

*Opposite: dining in
a shopping mall*

In the home of the bean and the cod, don't expect to find much of either. Boston baked beans long ago joined chicken *à la* king as endangered American food species. Cod that once were thick enough in the ocean waters off the Massachusetts coast to be caught in baskets have all but disappeared from over-fishing. Likewise, New England boiled dinner of corned beef and cabbage is a rarity served only on St Patrick's Day.

New England fare

The contemporary selection of fresh seafood available in most restaurants includes monkfish, red snapper and Arctic char, among others. What hasn't changed is that a visit to Boston still isn't complete without a bowl of clam chowder and a boiled lobster. Otherwise, the culinary possibilities are virtually endless, from pasta to pad thai, burgers to burritos, and steak to sushi.

The microbrewing revolution that swept America in the last decade began in Boston and appropriately was sparked by Samuel Adams, 'patriot-brewer.' Today, ales and lagers with the 'Sam Adams' label are ubiquitous at city restaurants and bars. A half dozen 'brew pubs' scattered around Boston and Cambridge offer up a variety fresh beer on tap to help wash down generous plates of hearty pub grub.

61

Restaurants

$$$ expensive ($25 or more per person); $$ moderate ($15-25 per person); $ inexpensive (under $15 per person). Prices do not include wine, tax, and gratuities (it's customary to tip 15% of the total bill). Whatever the night or season, reservations are recommended, although not all restaurants will accept them, particularly on weekends.

Eating at leisure...

...and on the run

Ambrosia, 116 Huntington Ave. (tel: 247-2400) Anthony Ambrose juxtaposes Asian spices with native seafood and calls on his travels in France and his work experience there with Japanese chefs. $$$
Aujourd'hui, Four Seasons Hotel, 200 Boylston Street (tel: 338-4400). Formal atmosphere for fine Continental and creative American cuisine. Elegant setting overlooking Public Garden. $$$
Biba, 272 Boylston Street (tel: 426-7878). Lydia Shire's showcase for contemporary cuisine. $$$
Bob The Chef's, 604 Columbus Avenue (tel: 536-6204). Southern cuisine and atmosphere. $
Brew Moon, 115 Stuart Street/City Place (tel: 523-6467). Casual, contemporary atmosphere. On-site microbrewery and American cuisine. $$
Cornucopia on the Waterfront, 100 Atlantic Avenue (tel: 367-0300). Traditional New England seafood and new American cuisine with harbor view. $$

Local brews are popular

Eating out on Newbury Street

Dom's, 10 Bartlett Street (tel: 367-8979). A North End landmark, memorable for Italian owner Dominic Caposella's habit of sitting with patrons as they order.

Durgin-Park, Faneuil Hall Marketplace, North Market (tel: 227-2038). A landmark. Try scrod and chowder. $

Dynasty, 33 Edinboro Street, (tel: 350-7777) Chinatown's most popular dim sum served early on Sunday. $

Legal Sea Foods, Park Plaza Hotel, 135 Columbus Avenue, and other downtown locations. Good seafood. $$

Locke-Ober, 3-Winter Place (tel: 542-1340). Established in 1875 and still serving American classics such as Oysters Rockefeller, Lobster Savannah, and Indian pudding. Jacket and tie required. $$$

Maison Robert, 45 School Street (tel: 227-3370). Elegant formal dining room serving French and American cuisine; summer outdoor terrace. $$$

Morton's of Chicago, One Exeter Place (tel: 266-5858). Prime dry-aged beef and chops, fresh seafood. Extensive wine list. $$$.

Olive's, 10 City Square, Charlestown. Mediterranean cuisine from much-admired chef Todd English. $$$

Pignoli, 79 Park Square (tel: 338-7500). Wide-ranging selection of creatively-prepared Italian cuisine. $$$

Rowes Wharf Restaurant, Boston Harbor Hotel, 70 Rowes Wharf on Atlantic Avenue (tel: 439-3995). Fascinating blend of regional and native cuisine. $$$

Seasons Restaurant, Bostonian Hotel at Faneuil Hall Marketplace (tel: 523-4119). Inventive American cuisine in rooftop setting overlooking marketplace. $$$

St Botolph Restaurant, 99 St. Botolph Street (tel: 266-3030). Continental food in a charmingly restored 19th-century townhouse. $$

Turner Fisheries Bar & Restaurant, 10 Huntington Avenue (tel: 424-7425). In Westin Hotel. Try oysters. $$$

Ye Olde Union Oyster House, 41 Union Street (tel: 227-2750). America's oldest restaurant, established 1826, serving traditional New England seafood. $$

Cambridge

Elephant Walk, 70 Union Square, Somerville (tel: 623-9939). Praised for French and Cambodian cuisine. $$

Grendel's Den, 89 Winthrop Street (Tel: 491-1160) with working fireplace in winter. $

Harvest, 44 Brattle Street (tel: 492-1115). Specializes in native New England game. $$$

John Harvard Brew House, 33 Dunster Street (tel: 868-3585). Restaurant-cum-brewery. Good pub food. $$

Rialto, Charles Hotel, One Bennett Street (tel: 661-5050). Regional cuisine with flair. Supper club ambience. $$$

Salamander, One Atheneum Street (tel: 225-2121). Wood grille dishes unusually prepared with an Asian accent. $$$

Shopping

In the Victorian era, 'proper Bostonians' were notorious for thrift, disregard for fashion, and general lack of acquisitiveness. Their ranks have since thinned considerably, however. Today, one can spend freely while shopping throughout the Boston area and satisfy just about any taste, cosmopolitan and otherwise. There is no lack of souvenirs either for visitors wanting to bring a bit of Boston home.

Shop till you drop

Downtown Crossing (Washington Street)

When Edward Filene opened **Filene's Automatic Bargain Basement** in 1909, fellow merchants wondered if he'd lost his mind. Any item on the shelves that didn't sell immediately was discounted over several weeks until it was either sold or given away. Filene's Basement was not profitable for 10 years, but it has done rather well ever since. For special sales 'in the basement,' eager shoppers gather long before doors open. **Filene's**, a traditional department store, is located on several floors above.

Across a pedestrian-only section of Summer Street, **Macy's** (formerly Jordan Marsh) is the competition. It's a quick hop from Macy's to the **Brattle Book Shop**, 9 West Street, the nation's oldest bookseller, which sells rare and used books. In the immediate area are numerous jewelers as well as what is supposedly the world's largest **Woolworth's**.

Faneuil Hall Marketplace/Marketplace Center

In three restored buildings from the 19th-century, **North Market, South Market** and the colonnaded **Quincy Market**, and **Marketplace Center**, an adjacent modern retail/office tower, can be found just about everything to eat, drink, wear or read at over 150 specialty shops and 22 restaurants. Before the area was re-created as a 'festival marketplace' in the mid-1970s, it had served as a center of merchant activity for a century and a half. Over time, the Faneuil Hall Marketplace has come to resemble an ordinary shopping mall within an extraordinary historic setting. Shops include Waterstone's, the Disney Store, and the Celtic Weaver, specializing in handmade Irish sweaters and clothing. **Bull Market** pushcarts showcase the colorful wares of over 100 New England artisans and entrepreneurs.

Faneuil Hall Marketplace

Newbury Street

'Rodeo Drive East' stretches from Arlington Street at the Ritz Carlton to the **Tower Records** building at Massachusetts Avenue. From wealthy international students to aspiring rock stars, Newbury Street affords some of the best people-watching in Boston and plenty of sidewalk

Newbury Street hemlines

cafés encourage the sport. As one walks west, the shops gradually shift from chic (**Giorgio Armani Boutique**, 22 Newbury Street) to cheap (**Mystery Train Records**, 306 Newbury Street, has a thorough selection of 'recycled' music).

The city's **art galleries** congregate here, as well as the **Society of Arts & Crafts**, 175 Newbury Street, featuring jewelry and furniture by local artisans. **Gargoyles, Grotesques & Chimeras**, 262 Newbury Street, sells artfully-rendered reproduction statues, and **Allston Beat**, 348 Newbury Street, is a clothing store favored by the city's alternative crowd. The café at **Sonsie Restaurant**, 327 Newbury, aspires to Parisian sophistication, while across the street, **Trident Bookseller & Cafe**, 338 Newbury Street, caters to New Age interests.

Ethnic inscriptions

Prudential Center

Copley Place/Shops at Prudential Center

You can shop till you drop and never worry about the raindrops in this sprawling indoor mall complex near Copley Square. Walkways connect to various buildings, including the Hynes Convention Center. **Neiman Marcus** and **Saks Fifth Avenue** department stores are among more than 100 merchants and food purveyors.

Cambridge

HMV Records and the Gap might be found almost anywhere, but in the intellectual hothouse of **Harvard Square**, their neighbors include **Schoenhof's Foreign Books**, 76A Mt Auburn Street, the area's finest international bookseller, and the **Cambridge Artists Cooperative**, 59A Church Street, selling jewelry, clothing, pottery and crafts by local artisans. For Harvard College souvenirs, the **Harvard Cooperative Society** has a wide selection of sweatshirts, caps, T-shirts and ties. For mall-hoppers, the **Shops at Charles Place** (adjacent to the Charles Hotel) and the **Cambridgeside Galleria** near the Museum of Science have the usual assortment of department and specialty stores.

Antiques

If proper Bostonians weren't terribly enamored of fashion, they were decidedly fond of outfitting their homes with fine furniture and artworks. What hasn't been passed down through the generations frequently ends up in local antique shops. **Boston Antique Co-op**, 119 Charles Street (tel: 227-9810), is one of many such specialty stores in the Beacon Hill area.

Between the North End and the FleetCenter sports arena, **Boston Antique Center**, 54 Canal Street (tel: 742-1400) houses 50 dealers on three selling floors and will arrange shipping worldwide.

Charles Street store

Nightlife

The Boston beat

The rap on Boston for visitors is that it's a daylight-hours-only attraction. After you've walked the Freedom Trail all afternoon, goes the thinking, there's nothing else to do. In fact, with all those resident students and twenty-some-things to amuse when they've put down the books or left the office, Boston has ample night-time diversions.

Clubs
Alley Cat Lounge, One Boylston Place (tel: 451-6200), with CD jukebox and large-screen television. **Avalon**, 15 Landsdowne Street (tel: 262-2424), with state of the art light and sound system. **Bill's Bar & Lounge**, 5 Lands-downe Street (tel: 421-9678), low-key bar with 1960s retro feel. **QUEST**, 1270 Boylston Street (tel: 424-7747), four-story nightclub and Boston's only roofdeck bar. **Venus de Milo**, 11 Landsdowne Street (tel: 421-9595), Roman gothic ballroom style club features modern dance groove music. **Zanzibar**, One Boylston Place (tel: 351-2560), hottest tropical nightspot features a decor of soaring palm trees and authentic Caribbean architecture.

Dancing the night away

Comedy
Boston's celebrated comedy clubs feature both locals and national stars.
Comedy Connection, Quincy Market, Upper Rotunda (tel: 248-9700) was voted 'Best Comedy Club in the Coun-try' by *USA Today*. **Nick's Comedy Stop**, 100 Warren-ton Street (tel: 482-0930).

Film
Boston Film-Video Foundation, 1126 Boylston Street (tel: 536-1540 highlights work by avant-garde filmmak-ers. **Coolidge Corner Theatre**, 290 Harvard Street,

Brookline (tel: 734-2500), a superb 'art film' house in an Art Deco setting. **Harvard Film Archive**, 24 Quincy Street, Carpenter Center for the Visual Arts, Harvard University (tel: 495-4700) shows contemporary and classic art films from around the world. **Kendall Square Cinema**, One Kendall Square, Cambridge (tel: 494-9800) and **Nickelodeon Cinemas**, 606 Commonwealth Avenue, Boston (tel: 424-1500) feature off-beat, first-run films.

Folk
Passim Coffee Shop & Gallery, 47 Palmer Street, Cambridge (tel: 492-7679) is a journey back to the hippy heyday of Harvard Square.

Jazz
Boston's two major venues for top-notch jazz artists compete from opposite sides of the Charles River. **The Regattabar**, Charles Hotel, One Bennett Street, Cambridge (tel: 661-5000) brings greats from McCoy Tyner to local diva Rebecca Parris to the heart of Harvard Square. **Scullers**, DoubleTree Guest Suites-Boston/Cambridge, 400 Soldiers Field Road (tel: 783-0090. River views and good vibes. Aficionados will seek out emerging artists in Inman Square, Cambridge (10 minutes from Harvard Square) at **Ryles**, 212 Hampshire Street (tel: 876-9330).

Hot jazz on a cool summer night

66

Rock/Blues
Rock supergroups such as Aerosmith and the Cars first won attention in Boston clubs. At **Hard Rock Cafe**, 131 Clarendon Street (tel: 424-7625, such talismans as a pink-and-black 'Candy-O' jacket worn by Cars' leader Ric Ocasek and Joe Perry's blue suede boots make up the inspirational backdrop for numerous local acts aspiring to follow their lead. Not ones to forget their roots in small Boston clubs, members of the arena-rocking Aerosmith recently opened **Mama Kin**, 36 Landsdowne Street (tel: 536-2100) to provide local rockers a nurturing venue. Mama Kin neighbor **Avalon**, 15 Landsdowne Street (tel: 262-2424) also hosts up-and-coming bands.

Aerosmith played here

A short walk away in Kenmore Square, **The Rathskeller** (everyone calls it 'the Rat'), 528 Commonwealth Avenue (tel: 536-2750) has weathered trends from punk to grunge and has the scars to prove it. **The Paradise**, 967 Commonwealth Avenue (tel: 562-8804) is a time-honored home for rock and blues. **Sticky Mike's**, 21 Boylston Place (tel: 351-2583) specializes in blues in the Theatre District. In Harvard Square, **House of Blues**, 96 Winthrop Street (tel: 491-2583) has a popular Sunday gospel brunch.

In Cambridge at Central Square, the **Middle East Restaurant**, 472 Massachusetts Avenue (tel: 492-9181) showcases wide range of alternative and progressive rock.

Activities

Bicycling

Those willing to brave the traffic on two wheels will enjoy pedaling by the Charles River following the **Dr Paul Dudley White Bikeway**. The Bicycle Coalition of Massachusetts, 214A Broadway, Cambridge, MA 02139 (tel: 491-7433) has information and maps.

Beating the traffic

Billiards

'Pool' is suddenly hip. **Jillian's Billiard Club**, 145 Ipswich St., (tel: 437-0300) and the **Boston Billiard Club**, 126 Brookline Ave., (tel: 536-7665) are popular gathering spots in the Kenmore Square Fenway area.

Birdwatching

One of the country's oldest environmental organizations, the **Massachusetts Audubon Society**, 208 South Great Road, Lincoln, MA 01773 (tel: 259-9500), manages several wildlife sanctuaries in the greater Boston area.

67

Speed king

Jogging/Rollerblading

Runners congregate on paths along the Boston and Cambridge banks of the Charles River as well as trails through the Emerald Necklace chain of parks. On summer Sundays from 11am to 7pm, Memorial Drive from Eliot Bridge is conveniently closed to vehicles. These days, runners share the lanes with rollerbladers on in-line skates; **Beacon Hill Skate Shop**, 135 Charles Street, (tel: 482-7400), rents equipment and safety gear.

Parks

Boston's major green spaces include the sprawling **Arnold Arboretum**, 125 Arborway, Jamaica Plain (tel: 524-1717),

Blade-runners by the Charles

Lazing in the Public Garden

home to more than 7,000 kinds of trees and shrubs, and the **Back Bay Fens** (behind the Museum of Fine Arts). Both are part of the **Emerald Necklace** chain designed by the landscape architect Frederick Law Olmsted that runs from the **Public Garden** to **Franklin Park** (for information, contact the city's Parks and Recreation Dept., tel: 635-4505). In the 1880s, Olmsted, who had been superintendant of New York's Central Park, imposed a vision for landscape design and preserving open space. His governing principles were scenery, suitability, sanitation, subordination, separation, and spaciousness.

For refreshing ocean air, visit **Castle Island Park**, site of Fort Independence, in South Boston, where Edgar Allen Poe served with the army and found inspiration for his tale, *The Cask of Amontillado*. From May to October, take a ferry (no cars) from Long Wharf (Bay State Cruises, tel: 723-7800) to **Boston Harbor Islands State Park**.

Sailing
On the Charles River, between the Hatch Shell and Charles Street pedestrian, **Community Boating** (tel: 523-1038) has weekly memberships for qualified boaters. Staff at the **Boston Sailing Center**, 54 Lewis Wharf (tel: 227-4198), take groups of up to six for an hour's sail in the harbor.

Skating
The lagoon at the **Public Garden** is the city's premier skating spot in winter. The town of Brookline also operates a public outdoor rink at **Larz Anderson Park**, 253 Newton Street (tel: 730-2080).

Spectator Sports
Baseball: the American League **Boston Red Sox** (tel: 267-1700) play at Fenway Park, the nation's oldest professional

Sailing into Gloucester

diamond, from April to September. Fenway opened in 1912, but its most distinguishing feature – a 37-ft wall behind left field known as the 'Green Monster,' wasn't built until 1934. The park's first season saw the Sox win the World Series – a trick they haven't managed since 1918.

Basketball: the National Basketball Association **Boston Celtics** (tel: 523-3030) play at the new FleetCenter, on Causeway Street beside North Station, October to May.

Tomorrow's champions

Running: first organized in 1897 by the Boston Athletic Association (tel: 236-1652), the **Boston Marathon** is nation's oldest and attracts the world's finest runners to race over the official Olympic distance of 26 miles and 365 yards on the third Monday in April (Patriot's Day, a state holiday). 8,000 participants, 1½ million spectators.

Football: on eight Sundays between September and December the **New England Patriots** (tel: 1-800-543-1776) of the National Football League play home games at Foxboro Stadium (25 miles from downtown, accessible by commuter rail). Local college teams playing in the city on intermittent Saturday afternoons in the fall include the **Boston College Eagles**, Alumni Stadium, Chestnut Hill (tel: 552-3000); **Boston University Terriers**, Nickerson Field, Brighton (tel: 353-3838); and **Harvard University Crimson**, Harvard Stadium, North Harvard Street, Allston (tel: 495-2211).

69

Hockey: the **Boston Bruins** (tel: 624-1000) of the National Hockey League skate the FleetCenter ice from October to May.

Rowing: in mid-October, the annual **Head of the Charles Regatta** on the Charles River draws thousands of college teams for the world's largest, single-day crew racing event. Competing boats set off, one after the other, at brief intervals and are timed over the course.

Soccer: yet another attempt is underway to bring professional soccer – 'football' to Europeans – to American audiences; the **New England Revolution** (tel: 508-543-0350; 1-800-543-1776) of Major League Soccer play at Foxboro Stadium in spring and summer.

Traveling down the Charles

Tennis: the **US Pro Tennis Championships** are played on the hard courts of the Longwood Cricket Club, 564 Hammond Street, Brookline (tel: 731-2900) during the second week in July.

Whale Watches

A half dozen species of whales inhabit the Stellwagen Bank, a protected maritime sanctuary between Cape Ann and Cape Cod some 15 miles offshore from Boston. Trips take five hours or more, and run daily from April through September. Operators include **New England Aquarium Whale Watch** (tel: 973-5277), **A.C. Cruise Line** (tel: 261-6633), and **Boston Harbor Whale Watch** (tel: 345-9866).

Getting There

By air

Logan International Airport, 2 miles from downtown in Boston Harbor, has five terminals (A–E). International flights arrive at Terminal E. Free 24-hour inter-terminal shuttle bus. For news of traffic conditions between town and airport, call **Massport's Ground Transportation Hotline** (1-800-235-6426), Monday–Friday, 8am–7pm.

At Airport Station, the MBTA Blue Line connects Logan to downtown in about 10 minutes (fare is $0.85). The **Airport Water Shuttle** (tel: 330-8680) has daily crossings from Logan to Rowes Wharf (Boston Harbor Hotel) in seven minutes (free shuttle bus operates between ferry dock and all airport terminals); peak period service is every 15 minutes, off-peak is half-hourly, and one-way fare is $8. For cab fare to downtown, expect to pay about $20, including tip and tolls.

By rail

Amtrak's Northeast Corridor passenger service (NYC, Washington DC etc) begins and ends at Boston's South Station (Atlantic Avenue and Summer Street; tel:482-3660; 1-800-872-7245 or, for hearing-impaired, 1-800-523-6590). South Station also is eastern terminus for Amtrak's Lake Shore Limited (Chicago etc). In addition, all trains stop at Back Bay Station (tel: 722-3200).

By bus (coach)

Boston's sleek new bus terminal recently opened at South Station. **Greyhound** (tel:1-800-231-2222), **Peter Pan** (tel: 1-800-343-9999) and **Bonanza** (tel: 720-4110, 1-800-556-3815) have frequent express service to New York City (under five hours) and points in New England. Greyhound and Peter Pan also have terminals at Riverside Station on the MBTA Green Line 'D' branch.

By car

From the west: Route 90 (Mass. Turnpike) has three major city exits — Exits 18-20, Cambridge/Allston (best for Cambridge); Exit 22, Prudential Center/Copley Square (best for Back Bay); and Exit 24 (best for downtown).

From the south: Routes 95, 24 and 3 all feed into Route 128 East, which leads to Route 93 North. Two major exits are Kneeland Street/Chinatown (best for Back Bay, Theatre District), and Dock Square (best for Airport, North End, Waterfront and Faneuil Hall Marketplace).

From the north: Routes 1, 93, and 95 enter Boston. Major exits are: Storrow Drive (best for Back Bay and Beacon Hill); High Street (best for downtown); and Kneeland Street (best for Chinatown and Theatre District).

They're not joking

Getting Around

Boston's compact size, good public transportation system, notorious drivers, and confusing streetscape are reasons for hoofing it or hopping on a train. If you must drive, don't expect to find a parking space on the streets, and if you use a garage or car park expect to pay top dollar.

Car rental

All set

Most major rental companies have locations at Logan Airport and downtown. Alamo 1-800-327-9633; Avis, 1-800-331-1212; Budget, 1-800-527-0700; Enterprise, 236-6979; Hertz,1-800-654-3131; National, 1-800-227-7368

Rapid transit

Trains: The Massachusetts Bay Transit Authority – known as 'the T' by residents – operates four rapid transit lines (Red, Green, Orange and Blue) that intersect in the downtown area and run between 5am and 1am daily. 'Inbound' means toward downtown; 'outbound' means away from downtown. Green line 'subway' cars (trams) travel on four different branches above and below ground: B-Boston College (Commonwealth Avenue, past Boston University); C-Cleveland Circle (Beacon Street via Kenmore Square and Coolidge Corner); D-Riverside (mostly through suburban Brookline and Newton); and E-Heath Street or Arborway (past Museum of Fine Arts, Mass. College of Art, and Northeastern University). Tokens ($0.85) are necessary at all underground stations; above ground, tokens or exact change are accepted. A MBTA 'Boston Passport' allows three days' unlimited travel on buses and trains for $9 (seven days, $18). Information, tel: 722-3200.

72

Rapid transit

Buses: Route 1 runs along Massachusetts Avenue from Back Bay, across the Charles River, to MIT and Harvard Square. Otherwise, buses are rarely used in the city center. Fare is $0.60 and exact change is required.

Commuter Rail: Trains from **North Station** (Causeway Street beside Fleet Center, on Green and Orange Lines) and **South Station** (Summer Avenue and Atlantic Avenue, on Red Line) serve many popular tourist destinations such as Concord, Salem, Lowell, and Rockport. Tickets may be purchased at stations or on board, subject to a surcharge.

Taxis

Rather than trying to hail a cab, especially in poor weather, search out a taxi stand outside a hotel: Tolls at bridges and tunnels are charged to the rider, but there is no extra charge for more than one passenger. Outside a 12-mile radius of downtown, a flat fee is charged.

Facts for the Visitor

Service with a smile

Tourist information

Boston Common Visitor Information Center, on Tremont Street (perpendicular to West Street) is a treasure trove of free maps, brochures and information on greater Boston destinations. Open daily from 9am to 5 pm.
National Park Service Visitor Center, 15 State Street (tel: 242-5642), is open daily 9am to 5 pm.
Greater Boston Convention and Visitors Bureau (tel: 1-800-888-5515) provides visitor information Monday through Friday, 9am to 5pm. Boston By Phone is a similar 24-hour service, tel: 1-800-374-7400.

Foreign currency exchange

Convenient brokers include **Thomas Cook Currency Services**, 160 Franklin Street (tel: 1-800-223-9392); **American Express Travel Service,** One Court Street (tel: 723-8400); and numerous **BankBoston** branch offices in Boston and Cambridge (tel: 788-5000). Logan Airport's Terminal E has a convenient exchange counter.

Sightseeing tours

In this 'walking city,' pedestrian tours by **Boston By Foot** (tel: 367-2345) are especially popular. **Beantown Trolley** (tel: 236-2148), **Old Town Trolley** (tel: 269-7010) and the **Blue Trolley** (tel: 876-5539) are actually creatively-fashioned buses that board at hotels and other locations and circulate around major downtown attractions; they'll com-

Touring by trolley

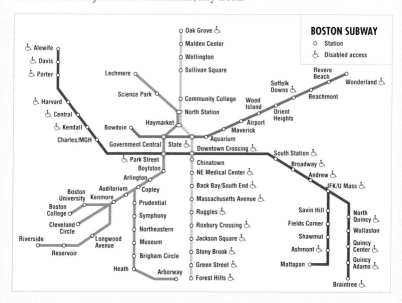

pete fiercely for your custom. **Boston Duck Tours** (tel: 723-3825) ride the city's streets in authentic World War II amphibious vehicles, then make a brief water-bound detour into the Charles River. **Don Quijote Tours** (tel: 236-1555) offers tours in Spanish and Portuguese.

Post offices

The General Mail Facility or main post office is at 25 Dorchester Avenue, behind South Station, is open 24 hours (tel: 451-9922 for general information). The Post Office at Logan Airport, 139 Harborside Drive, (tel: 567-1090) is also open 24 hours.

Opening times/Business hours

Keeping in touch

Most offices are open Monday to Friday, 9am to 5pm, although some open at 8am. Shops are generally open daily from 9am to 6 pm, though some open at 10am and stay open later; on Sundays, most stores open at noon. Banks are open Monday to Friday 9am to 4pm, and often later; Saturday hours are usually 9am to 2pm. With the exception of Thanksgiving (last Thursday in November), Christmas and New Year's Day, shops, restaurants and other commercial establishments are open seven days a week.

Emergencies

In Boston and Cambridge, dial 911 (toll-free) for police and fire emergencies.

Disabled

The City of Boston's Disabled Persons Commission can be reached at tel: 635-3682.

Visas & passports

A valid passport is required to enter the United States. Visas are required for some nationalities. Vaccinations are not required.

Health

Health care in the United States is very expensive and foreign visitors are advised to obtain health insurance before leaving home.

Money matters

American Express and Visa are the most readily accepted traveler's checks. American Express, Visa, MasterCard and Diners Club credit cards are widely honored, too, but be sure to ask waiters and clerks before you order dinner or have your purchases tallied up. Be discreet when using credit cards in public; fraudsters may be watching or listening as you use your card in a phone call. To transfer money, call Western Union (tel: 1-800-325-6000).

What to wear

Like most Americans, Bostonians prefer to dress as casually as possible. A very few restaurants and hotels require 'jacket and tie' – the mayor was once refused entrance to the Ritz-Carlton. Some clubs and bars prohibit sneakers and T-shirts.

Informality rules

Time zones

Boston is on Eastern Standard Time (Greenwich Mean Time minus five hours). From the first Sunday in April until the last Sunday in October, the clock is moved forward one hour for Daylight Savings Time. Boston is one hour ahead of Chicago; three hours ahead of Los Angeles; five hours behind London; and 15 hours behind Tokyo.

Climate

Part of Boston's magic is that it is a place of distinctive seasons. The summer months – June until mid-September – can be very hot and humid, although for much of the time the temperature keeps within an agreeable 70° to 80°F (21° to 27°C). In fall, the region is ablaze with colorful foliage and temperatures begin to drop, especially at night. Winter months, between November and March, are cold, windy and frequently snowy. The Charles River usually freezes over. Spring arrives in April and May with pleasant, sunny days and occasional heavy rains. For the latest weather reports, call 936-1234.

The heat's on

75

Newspapers

Boston's daily papers are the *Globe* and *Herald*; on Thursday, the *Globe*'s 'Calendar' pull-out section lists the area's cultural activities. The *Christian Science Monitor*, a prestigious newspaper published in Boston on weekdays, majors on international rather than local news. The Boston *Phoenix*, an arts and culture weekly, is published on Thursdays. For national and international newspapers and magazines, visit **Out of Town News** (tel: 354-7777) in Harvard Square beside the Red Line T station entrance.

News from everywhere

Radio & Television

Radio stations in the area include: WBNW on 590AM for business news; WRKO on 680AM for talk; WEEI on 850AM for sports; WCRB on 102.5FM for classical music; WBCN on 104.1FM for rock music; WGBH (Public Radio) on 89.7FM for classical music and jazz; andWBUR (National Public Radio) on 90.9FM for news.

Television stations include Channel 2 (WGBH) for Public Television; Channel 25 (WXNE) for Fox; and Channel 38 (WSBK) for sports. National networks can be viewed on Channel 4 (WBZ) for CBS, Channel 5 (WCVB) for ABC, and Channel 7 (WNEV) for NBC.

'Make Way for Ducklings'

Boston with Children

From the swan boats at the Public Garden to the petting zoo at Franklin Park Zoo, Boston abounds with activities of special interest to children.

Youngsters are welcome at all public attractions and even museums primarily of interest to adults make an effort to add 'fun' to otherwise intellectually-oriented exhibits. The **Museum of Fine Arts**, for example, provides an activity booklet for 'an art adventure' throughout its galleries (children will be mesmerized by the superb collection of Egyptian mummies). Energetic young travelers waiting for their flights can even romp in the **Logan Airport Kidport** play area at Terminal C.

The enduring popularity of Robert McCloskey's *Make Way for Ducklings* book, set in the **Public Garden**, makes a stop there a must. In addition to riding the **swan boats** (daily April to September, 10am to 5pm) for a chance to feed the lagoon's resident ducks, small children will want to meet the Mallard family – bronze statues of a duck and eight ducklings, perfect for climbing on – located at the corner of Charles Street and Beacon Street.

Boston's **Children's Museum**, 300 Congress Street (tel: 426-6500), encourages children to play, dress up, and pretend. Exhibits include a full-scale reconstruction of a typical Japanese home and a climbing apparatus for older kids. Directly beside it, the world's only **Computer Museum** (tel: 426-2800) offers video games, an over-sized Walk-Thru Computer, and a gallery of robots and 'smart' machines including the original R2-D2 from *Star Wars*.

Children's Museum
New England Aquarium

At the **New England Aquarium**, Central Wharf opposite Faneuil Hall Marketplace (tel: 973-5200), a special room for children lets them touch and hold starfish and horseshoe crab. It's almost always dinner time for penguins, sharks, rays and and other resident sea creatures.

In the Charles Hayden Planetarium at the **Museum of Science**, Science Park (tel: 723-2500), a multi-media 'starship ride' takes specators on a galactic tour; other exhibits include a 20-ft high Tyrannosaurus Rex dinosaur; a child-focused Discovery Center; and the Mugar Omni Theatre with 'wrap-around' screen and sound. Two hundred yards away in the Cambridgeside Galleria Mall, the **Sports Museum of New England** (tel: 577-7678) lets kids measure up to a life-size statue of Celtics basketball star Larry Bird and get behind home plate to catch for Red Sox baseball pitching ace Roger Clemens.

At the terminus of the Emerald Necklace, the **Franklin Park Zoo**, One Franklin Park Road (tel: 442-2002), lets kids get close to a Scottish highland cow and green iguana, among others; the gorillas in the African Tropical Forest exhibit, however, live behind plexiglass walls.

Where to Stay

Metropolitan Boston has well over 20,000 hotel rooms, but booking ahead is recommended, especially in summer and on holiday weekends in the fall. Large conventions can all but lock up the city's major downtown hotels.

For general information on accommodations and reservation services, call the Greater Boston Convention and Visitors Bureau toll-free hot line 1-800-888-5515, Monday through Friday, 9am to 5pm, or Boston By Phone, 1-800-374-7400, a 24-hour service.

Boston
$$$$ (over $200 per night double)
Boston Harbor Hotel, 70 Rowes Wharf, tel: 439-7000/ 1-800-752-7077. Boston's luxury waterfront hotel – the Airport Water Shuttle to Logan leaves from Rowes Wharf directly outside. All bedrooms have harbor or skyline views. **Bostonian Hotel**, at Faneuil Hall Marketplace, tel: 523-3600/ 1-800-343-0922. Directly opposite Faneuil Hall, the Bostonian is a modern brick structure at the edge of a dense warren of restaurants, grocery shops and butchers. **Copley Plaza Hotel**, 138 St. James Avenue, tel: 267-5300/1-800-822-4200). Located on Copley Square. Called 'the Grande Dame of Boston' for its opulent Old World architecture. **Four Seasons Hotel**, 200 Boylston Street, tel: 338-4400/1-800-332-3442. Overlooking the Public Garden, it was ranked fourth best US hotel in one poll. Complete health club with a lap pool, complimentary downtown limousine, and award-winning Aujourd'hui restaurant. **Le Meridien**, 250 Franklin Street, tel: 451-1900/1-800-543-4300. In the central Financial District at Post Office Square Park, Boston's newest downtown green space and a popular picnic spot in summer with nearby office workers. **Ritz-Carlton**, 15 Arlington Street, tel: 536-5700/1-800-241-3333. A symbol of Boston's graciousness and elegance since the 1927, when it was the nation's first Ritz. Two staff members for every guest. Restaurant, lounge and many bedrooms overlook Public Garden. **Sheraton Boston Hotel & Towers**, 39 Dalton Street, tel: 236-2000/1-800-325-3535. With 1,250 rooms, New England's largest hotel: Separate 'Towers' section features butler service. Indoor walking paths connect to Hynes Convention Center and Prudential Center and Copley Place malls. **Swissotel Boston**, 1 Avenue de Lafayette, tel: 451-2600/1-800-621-9200. European luxury hotel in Financial District. **Westin Hotel**, 10 Huntington Avenue, tel: 262-9600, toll-free 1-800-228-3000. Boston's tallest hotel with more than 800 rooms, pool and health club, and three restaurants. Attached to Copley Place and Prudential Center shopping malls.

Ritzy food

The Long Wharf Marriot

Reception at the Lenox

$$$ ($150–200 per night double)

Back Bay Hilton Hotel, 40 Dalton Street, tel: 236-1100/ 1-800-874-0663. Boston's only downtown Hilton, near Prudential Center and Christian Science Complex, has been renovated. Boodles's Restaurant and Bar serves over 100 beers from American 'microbreweries.' **Boston Marriott Hotel Copley Place**, 110 Huntington Avenue, tel: 236-5800/1-800-228-9290. On edge of Copley Square and Back Bay with indoor pool and health club. **Boston Marriott Hotel Long Wharf**, 296 State Street, tel: 227-0800/1-800-228-9290. Beside New England Aquarium and across from Faneuil Hall Marketplace on historic Long Wharf. **Boston Park Plaza Hotel & Towers**, 64 Arlington Street, tel: 426-2000/1-800-225-2008. In Back Bay near Public Garden and Theatre District. Exercise and fitness center. Six restaurants, one bar. **Colonnade Hotel**, 120 Huntington Avenue, tel: 424-7000/1-800-962-3030. Opposite Christian Science Complex and Prudential Center. L-shaped rooms have distinct sitting, sleeping and dressing areas. Seasonal roof-top pool. **Copley Square Hotel**, 47 Huntington Avenue, tel: 536-9000/1-800-225-7062. Home of the award-winning Café Budapest and the Original Sports Saloon. Informal European-style hotel. **Lenox Hotel**, 710 Boylston Street, tel: 536-5300, toll-free 1-800-225-7676. Renovated guestrooms, many with working fireplaces. Close to shopping at Copley Place, Prudential Center and Newbury Street. Samuel Adams Brew House at street level. **Omni Parker House**, 60 School Street, tel: 227-8600. Where Parker House rolls were created and are still served. Claims to be oldest continually-operating hotel in America, though building dates from 1927. Malcolm X and Ho Chi Minh were once on the staff.

$$ ($100-150 per night double)

Tremont House, 275 Tremont Street, tel: 426-1400/1-800-331-9998. In the Theatre District and close to most attractions. An affordable downtown alternative

Cambridge

Charles Hotel $$$$, One Bennett Street, tel: 864-1200/reservations 1-800-882-1818. Harvard Square's only luxury hotel, overlooking Charles River. Elegant Rialto restaurant and Regattabar jazz bar. **DoubleTree Guest Suites-Boston/Cambridge** $$$, 400 Soldiers Field Road, tel: 783-0090/1-800-222-8733. Boston's only all-suite hotel, located on the Charles River at Storrow Drive (five-minute cab ride to Harvard Square); jazz nightly. **Inn at Harvard** $$$, 1201 Massachusetts Avenue, tel: 491-2222. At the gates of Harvard University with sunlit atrium dining room. **Sheraton Commander** $$-$$$, 16 Garden Street, tel: 547-4800/1-800-325-3535. Near Harvard and

Radcliffe. Some rooms have kitchenettes. Restaurant and café. **Harvard Square Hotel $$**, 110 Mount Auburn Street, tel: 864-5200/1-800-458-5886. In heart of Harvard Square and recently renovated.

Bed & Breakfast/Guest Houses
A room for two usually costs between $75 and $100.

Beacon Inn Guest Houses, 248 Newbury Street, tel: 266-7142. Kitchenette or refrigerator is provided in each room. **Bed & Breakfast Agency of Boston**, 47 Commercial Wharf, tel: 720-3540/1-800-248-9262. Downtown's largest selection of historic B&B homes including Federal and Victorian townhouses and beautifully restored 1840 waterfront lofts. **Bed & Breakfast–Cambridge & Greater Boston**, PO Box 1344, Cambridge, MA 02238, tel: 576-1492/1-800-888-0178. Charming B&Bs, homes and apartments; hosted and unhosted. **Eliot and Pickett Houses**, 25 Beacon Street, tel: 248-8707. At the top of Beacon Hill, both houses are brick townhouses with a total of 20 guest rooms. **463 Beacon Street Guest House**, tel: 536-1302. In turn-of-century brownstone near Charles River and Esplanade. Most rooms include kitchenette and private bath, cable TV. **Host Homes of Boston**, PO Box 117, Waban Branch, Boston, MA 02168, tel: 244-1308. A moored yacht in the harbor and a Victorian townhouse in the Back Bay are just some of the unusual listings. **Newbury Guest House**, 216 Newbury Street, tel: 437-7666. On Back Bay's busiest street for shopping and dining.

Classic accommodations

Concord
Colonial Inn $$-$$$, 48 Monument Square, tel: 508-369-9200

Gloucester
Vista Motel $-$$, 22 Thatcher Road, tel: 508-281-3410. Overlooking Good Harbor Beach, some rooms with balconies, kitchenettes. **Cape Ann Motor Inn $-$$**, 33 Rockport Road, tel: 508-281-2900. On Long Beach with balconies, kitchenettes.

Rockport
Addison Choate Inn $-$$, 49 Broadway, tel: 508-546-7543. Walk to town center, classic Yankee styling.

Salem
Hawthorne Hotel $$. On the Common, tel: 508-744-4080/1-800-729-7829. Period 18th-century reproduction furnishings, within walking distance of waterfront, museums, historic sites and shopping areas.

Sleeping in Salem

Index